From Work to Vocation

*A Philosophical Approach
to Work and Fulfillment*

by
Chris Farls
Patrick Cavanaugh Koroly

A Book by The Vocation Project

Published by The Vocation Project
3000 Village Run Rd
Ste 103, PMB 125
Wexford, PA 15090

Copyright © The Vocation Project, 2025
ISBN: 979-8-9998883-0-3

Cover design and book layout by Karen A. Mesaros

Foreword

Some of the most rewarding work I've done over my career was being a mentor to aspiring entrepreneurs. People at all stages of their careers, students, mid-career professionals, retirees, are curious to learn about how to start or buy a business for themselves. When I ask them "Why?", the answers are consistent: they want more freedom and control. They want to have a personal investment in their work: they're looking for something more.

But as we can all appreciate, there are circumstances and responsibilities in life that make it hard for most to take the risk and venture out on their own. I can teach them the mechanics of entrepreneurship, but it's their leap to make. Too often, work ends in frustration. For them, their life situation cannot accommodate the risks and sacrifices necessary for this profession. For me, I'm left searching for ways to help them find what they're looking for in their current situation, knowing their circumstances may never change.

This question has come to consume my thoughts post-retirement: how can we all come to realize those desires for freedom, control and ownership in our work, regardless of the job or profession? I co-founded The Vocation Project to conduct a lengthy exploration that combines real world entrepreneurial experience with a deep study of the human person.

This book is meant to share the discoveries we've made along the way. It is intended to be a reference to anyone, in any profession, at any stage in their career. We've looked to find principles that hold true for work and life. Our hope is that it becomes a resource to help you grow into the person you desire to be.

-Chris Farls

Introduction

In everything we do, we're looking to answer one fundamental question: what am I meant for? Every choice we make says something about what we believe life is meant for. We're always thinking about how to pursue happiness and purpose. Nobody can avoid these questions. We need answers just to go about our everyday lives. Even if you don't realize it, you are offering an answer with your actions.

These questions are often clearest in the context of work. We look to work to justify our lives. Work seems like such a crucial source of meaning for us—and yet it can still feel meaningless. At worst, it can seem to go against life's meaning: work can seem like an obstacle to life's real purpose. There's a disconnect between what we live for at work and what we live for the rest of the time.

We need an answer to this challenge. Too often, we choose thoughtless ways to handle these problems. There are many different approaches to these questions of happiness, fulfillment, and work. However, we decide to take shortcuts, emphasizing quick fixes over a deeper understanding. There's little concern for the process of finding the truth. We might know the how without knowing the why. Whether these answers work or not, we don't understand the truth behind them.

We want to offer more than just a quick answer. We want to work through the reasoning and evidence needed to understand these questions. Through this, we want to build a foundation that offers a tool to answer every question of happiness.

At its core, the question of happiness is a question of human nature. It's asking what's good or bad for a person. It's asking what leads to fulfillment. All of these questions can only be answered if we understand what drives us as people: what can we achieve as humans? What do we need, and what offers us real purpose?

We might try to look at these questions as simple problems of science or psychology. However, these approaches often lead to a reductive view of human nature. A scientific view relies on creating a clear set of laws that are always followed. It relies on gravity always working a certain way or molecules always combining in a certain way. In short, it relies on things being predictable.

Humans aren't predictable in this way. There are things that we do that can't be explained by any law. Although we can see certain trends and tendencies in humans, we cannot make definite predictions about people in the same way that we can about material things. Science and psychology are still useful tools, but they can't be our only way of asking about human nature.

Instead, we'll take a philosophical approach. Our goal is to use reason to look at human experience and find concepts and principles that are applicable to all human life. We cannot know for certain how people will react to different things. But we can still use the tools of philosophy to learn what a person is and what's good for us.

Our method takes inspiration from both ancient and modern philosophy. We were inspired by the tradition of philosophical dialogues, where thinkers started with basic assumptions and challenged them until they found a new answer. This method was meant to help find better answers and to help students work through these problems independently. We don't just want to show you the conclusions we've found. We want to show you the path we took to reach these answers.

This will be our method for answering these questions. Now, we'd like to outline the steps we'll take to help guide your reading.

First, we want to begin by understanding the source of the problem. It's common to feel a division between work and the rest of life. Often, we feel like we're living two lives, one at work and one at home. We struggle to feel like ourselves. We want to talk about this lack of integration and where it comes from. Through this book, we hope to look for a path to real integration.

These problems start with a misunderstanding of work. We need to understand what work means. Taking a viewpoint rooted in purpose, we want to show the unique human capacity for creativity and freedom.

But we also want to find work's inherent value. There's something in work worth taking pride in. We want to learn what it is that makes work worthwhile for its own sake. We also want to understand how this same value can apply to all of life, not just the workplace.

Each of these principles and values of work only has meaning within the context of each person's own story. The life you're meant to live isn't an abstract idea: everything that you're meant to do must make sense in the context of your life story. To this end, we want to offer some concrete ways to look at your life and understand the values this life story creates. What has made you the person you are? What drives you through everyday life? And what's the direction you're following?

But, as we'll learn, these rules that guide work can't just apply to one part of life. We need to learn how to bring these ideas beyond the workplace and into the rest of life in pursuit of a unified goal. We want to find a way to unite work and leisure: though we might think of them as opposites, we want to learn how they can cooperate and help bring each other to greater fulfillment. Each part of life should point in the same direction.

This choice of your goal and direction is the real meaning of freedom. In looking for a unified goal in life, we're looking for an opportunity to make an independent choice about what to pursue. This is the root of real integration and fulfillment.

With all this in mind, we'll finally offer a definition of vocation: work that brings together these concepts for a fulfilled and happy life. This is work that helps you achieve completeness in life, growing into the person you're meant to be.

How to Use This Book

Throughout this book, we'll look at many different philosophical concepts to discuss what makes work and life fulfilling and happy. Our goal isn't just to make these concepts easier to understand, but to help you see that you're capable of more than you thought. Some of these concepts are difficult. However, we've done our best to make them accessible through explanation and examples.

This is a book meant to be taken slowly. Our goal isn't just to offer a summary of our findings. We want to retrace the steps that led us to these ideas in the first place. At each step, we want you to be an active participant in this search. We encourage you to write notes, think about questions and challenges you might have, and try to join the argument yourself. This book is meant to be a conversation about these questions. We encourage you to try to speak back.

We also hope that this is an opportunity to talk about these ideas with those around you. It's best to think about all the different possible viewpoints on these questions. This book is best read with others. These questions should be answered by considering your own perspective and comparing it to other beliefs. Even if you're reading on your own, take the opportunity to ask others what they believe and see how they respond to the challenges we raise here.

This book is the product of decades of experience in the workplace and years of passionate study. Our goal is to offer a real picture of human happiness and fulfillment at work. More than just a chance to feel satisfied, we want to find what it means to live a complete life as a human being. We thank you for joining us on this search.

Acknowledgments

This book is the product of many conversations, debates, and lessons. We'd like to thank a few people for help in turning these ideas into a coherent whole: James Demasi, Grant Martsolf, Mike Aquilina, Jane Greer, and Matt Zagrocki. We'd also like to thank all the readers who've read our writings since the beginning. Your attention has been invaluable.

CONTENTS

Chapter 1

The Two Selves

*Why do we feel like we're living
as different people at work?*

There's a saying that often comes up when you hear someone complaining about a job: "I don't feel like myself at work." It's a common way to say that work is just missing something. We use it for all sorts of problems and frustrations.

We might say this thoughtlessly, like more of a small turn of phrase than anything substantial. We don't think of it as anything literal or part of some bigger philosophical problem. Just the same as we say metaphors like, "Work is killing me," or, "I'm sick of this," we don't use it to mean a specific thing.

But if we take a closer look, we can see that there's something more to this phrase than meets the eye. In one sense, it is just a metaphor for dissatisfaction. But without even thinking about it, it also leads us towards a deeper problem: we recognize a feeling of *disunity* between work and life. In some way, it feels as though each points in a different direction.

This is not just a metaphor. It brings us to the underlying problem that leads to dissatisfaction with work, life, or both. It reveals the most important obstacles to fulfillment.

How does this problem reveal itself? Where does it start in our everyday work?

The Roots of Unhappiness at Work

There are a thousand different reasons why we might feel unhappy at work. People often mention conflicts with coworkers, a lack of appreciation, or a lack of passion. Perhaps work is too stressful: it takes up too much of your time and energy. When facing this sort of problem, work becomes an obstacle to fulfillment. It can even become hard to see why we work in the first place.

We can think of a few examples and different underlying problems. A problem with your coworkers or your boss points to a problem with your fit in the workplace: you don't feel a sense of belonging. A lack of appreciation points to a feeling of disrespect: you aren't seeing the recognition you deserve. A lack of passion often points to a sense that your work isn't letting you live up to your potential: there's something you're capable of that you can't achieve in your work. Stress and a lack of time often show that work seems to demand too much of your life: somehow, it doesn't fit in with the rest of who you are.

All of these reflect something we need from a career. But each seems like a separate need that must be approached individually. It's hard to see what links a lack of passion with tension with your coworkers.

The root of the problem is the feeling that your work goes against *who you really are*. These issues start when it feels like you're living two separate lives: one at work and one at home. Whether you don't like your fit in the workplace, feel disrespected, think you're missing your potential, or feel like work takes the time needed for more important things, there's a feeling that the person who you *really* are is in conflict with the person you have to be for the sake of work.

The poet Walt Whitman said once, "Do I contradict myself? Very well then, I contradict myself. I contain multitudes." For him, it was a fact of life that we contain contradictions. We're not always sure who we're meant to be. It's not always clear how the different parts of life fit together. Our work selves and home selves aren't always easy to connect. Whitman felt confident accepting this. But for us, it might be harder to escape. We can't ignore work's impact on life: just putting it off to the side isn't an option.

At its core, this problem seems to begin with a feeling of *unfreedom*. The contradiction starts when we feel pulled towards one thing by nature but are forced to choose something else. We want to live one way, but work demands that we take a different path.

We gain a sense of identity through the free choices we make. We can't come to a complete understanding of ourselves by following the guardrails: we have to venture out on our own. Without that freedom, it's harder to identify yourself in your work. Suddenly, it seems like your work self and home self are serving totally different ends. You're leading two separate lives—and, unsurprisingly, neither feels complete.

Eventually, the person you are at work doesn't seem to have much in common with the person you are at home. Work and home are two separate lives with two separate directions, all lived by two selves. This is the source of these problems we saw before: we feel a contradiction between who we are forced to be at work and who we're really meant to be in life. We don't have an opportunity to make the choices we want.

When we're asking about unhappiness at work, this is where we need to start: we need to ask just what it is that makes these parts of life seem separate.

Importantly, we need to ask how to find that sense of freedom again. How can we find that choice within our work? What offers us a chance to make work our own and to fit it within the rest of life? To get past the separation between work and life, we need to figure out what they have in common.

To begin this search, we have a clear idea of just what we're after: we want to find a way to bring work and life together, united by a shared direction. In the end, we want to find what it means to lead a *complete* life. We should be able to recognize our full selves whether we're at work, at home, or anywhere else life might bring us.

Now, how can we begin to answer this question?

Using Your Full Self

It's hard to find an entry point for such a broad question. Let's ask a more concrete question: what is it that you're lacking when you don't feel like yourself at work?

Almost everybody has felt this sort of dissatisfaction at some point in life—we've all had that job we hate and can't wait to get out of. For many people, it's an everyday reality. Often, it seems that we aren't putting our full selves into our work. We feel like work requires us to live a fake life, putting on a certain persona to be someone we're not. There's a "work self" that's detached from the real self we know.

When this happens, we feel as though we can't live out our full potential. Strangely enough, it often seems like work can be the worst when it demands the least of us. It's harder to endure a full day of work that focuses on just one tiny part of you than a day of work that asks for your full self. This small part of yourself you're living through becomes exhausted and strained.

Before becoming a writer, David Foster Wallace was studying for his PhD in philosophy. He said that if he finished his degree, he likely would've worked at a think tank doing logical proofs for a living. Eventually, he decided to leave Harvard to focus on writing.

He was later asked why he decided to switch from philosophy to writing. In the end, he said, it came down to one thing: philosophy let him use 50% of himself while writing let him use 97% of himself.

This sense of using all of yourself (or nearly all, minus that 3%) seems to be the first thing we're looking for in the search for meaningful work. Work that we can check out from entirely rarely feels fulfilling. We shouldn't expect to find any reward from something we put nothing into. We're looking for work that seems to offer us a chance to be our full selves, not just a limited part.

But this pursuit isn't just looking for something that's more challenging or requires more of your skill. It also means looking for something that fits in with the rest of your life as well. Work isn't incomplete just because it demands too little of you: it's also important that it fits into living a complete life. The solution shouldn't just be harder work.

For many of us, both parts of this equation are lacking. It's common for work to feel monotonous and unengaging while also feeling overwhelming and difficult.

It's easy to just give up when facing these feelings. Plenty of people feel that they can't find meaningful work. Someone who sees no meaning in work will see no motivation to do it either. Why bother spending so much of your time on something that cannot bring you any real fulfillment?

Still, we work anyways. Regardless of whatever frustrations or difficulties we might have, we push on. Through discipline and willpower, we still overcome these problems. It doesn't matter how frustrating these problems get. We must have some kind of answer if we manage to get up and go to work in spite of these difficulties. Of course, this doesn't mean it's a satisfying solution: it may be a quick patch on a major issue.

If we want to find a lasting solution, our best starting point may be asking how we handle these problems already. It's a classic method in philosophy to begin by looking at the most common opinions on a question: we can start with a popular view and challenge that.

Let's ask, then: how do we approach these difficulties in practice, and how do our approaches fall short? There are two approaches in particular that might be illuminating for us and help to clarify some things about this problem. We'll call them the *grind mentality* and the *punch-out* mentality. These will show some of the mistakes we make in understanding work—and, hopefully, lead to a better answer.

The Grind Mentality

The grind mentality is simple: it says that real fulfillment comes from hard work for its own sake. Anyone who feels dissatisfied or lost at work is not working hard enough, and if you work harder, you can overcome these feelings. Never let your foot off the gas and you'll reach the finish line someday.

In the end, the goal is just to rise to the top and beat everyone else. Everything is part of a competition, and hard work is how you win. People advocating for this mentality might live luxuriously to try to show off their success, but the only thing really worth doing is hard work. In life, you're meant to rise above everybody else: your goal is the top of the mountain, and there's only room enough for one at the top.

Living this way, time spent away from work is wasted time. Anything that's not contributing to success is a mistake. Our goal, then, should be to work as much as possible and try to rest as little as we can.

If this is true, the only real thing that you need from work is the opportunity to work hard and be successful. It's the hardest workers who are *really* fulfilled. In the end, your life can be judged simply off whether you're lazy or hard-working.

For someone who feels that they lack a clear sense of identity, this approach offers a simple way to create one. Through hard work, it's possible to reinvent yourself and become whatever you want to be. Really, this mindset claims that you are *only* defined by your work.

We see this sort of mentality everywhere today. How often do we see people encouraging you to look at the whole world through the lens of work and competition? People try to frame friendship as 'networking' or hobbies as 'side-hustles.' Company cultures encourage 60- and 80-hour weeks. Everything goes back to your career.

What's the philosophy behind this response? Really, this idea is a literal application of the term *work ethic*: if you're working hard, then you're living right. If not, then you're living wrong. It's an easy philosophy to understand, though not so easy to follow. It's quickly clear that work alone isn't enough. These long hours and painful days blur together and lose any real direction.

In fact, this 'solution' is just a different version the original problem. There are still two identities in life: your work self and your resting self. No matter what, you can't eliminate this part of you that doesn't work. Now, instead of work feeling like your fake self, your personal life feels like your fake self.

In the end, reducing everything to work and success removes its meaning. What makes work valuable in the first place? The grind mentality can't quite explain this: it doesn't offer a reason why we should work hard. It says that hard work is good just because it's good. But this isn't a satisfying answer. We want to find work with purpose.

When we can't find this meaning in work, where do we turn? Perhaps the simplest response is to try reducing work's role in life. We look for an escape.

The Punch-Out Mentality
If the constant grind of work isn't enough to create meaning, what's our alternative? If we can't find a sense of identity

in work, we might decide to stop looking for one. Instead of looking for fulfillment in work, we can try to avoid it as much as possible.

We'll call this the *punch-out mentality*. If work isn't a path to meaning on its own, then it's simply meaningless. In this case, we should try to just avoid work as much as we can. When we punch in, we give up who we are. At work, we're forced to live as a fake version of ourselves, but when we punch out, we get to be who we truly are. All our dissatisfaction gets reduced to the fact that this fake self dominates so much of our lives.

We might think of this as the "working for the weekend" mentality. It reduces our "real life" to only those moments away from work where we aren't forced to fit into some place that we don't belong. All that we can do is try to maximize our time away from work and minimize our time wasted there.

You don't have to deny the existence of meaningful work to live this way. It's common to want work that's "real" or meaningful while thinking it's impossible to find. Perhaps some people can find meaningful work, but the average person has no hope of getting complete fulfillment from a job. In this view of things, work is just going to be an unfortunate roadblock to the really significant things in life.

Is it really the case that most of us have meaningless work? It seems that many people live this way. If work is nothing to you but an unfortunate evil that you devote eight hours of your day to, then you're living this way too.

Naturally, this leads to unhealthy coping as well. Some people might avoid friendships with coworkers to try to keep work from "invading" their lives. Others might binge TV or video games once they're off the clock to try to get out of the mindset of work. In any case, this doesn't get at the root of our dissatisfaction. If anything, it makes it worse.

Really, this approach makes the same mistake as the grind mentality. The grind mentality encourages us to see work as our real purpose and real source of identity. We're made for work and we're justified when we work. Under the punch-out mentality, our identity is what we are outside of work and work doesn't matter for understanding ourselves. It doesn't have anything to do with life's real meaning and offers nothing positive in our pursuit of meaning. In both cases, the goal is to focus on your "real" self in life and reduce the role of the less important part. Both *encourage* you to believe that your life is split between two selves.

There's a very simple response to the punch-out mentality: if work is "meaningless," then why do we do it? This might seem like a ridiculous question. Obviously, we work to survive. We work to make money and get by. For most people, that's the real meaning of work.

But we shouldn't act like this is an insignificant meaning. It might be an indirect path to achieving these goals, but it's a path nonetheless. Work might not be the center of our lives. It might not be something that we do for its own sake. But one thing should be clear: work is part of our *story*. Works builds to something greater. Ignoring it means cutting out a key part of what defines your everyday pursuit of happiness. We need to take all of life into account to understand fulfillment.

Both of these mentalities tried to divide life. They define us based on one small part of who we are. But defining ourselves based on one thing misses a major part of who we are. If we want to understand the value of work, we can't split life in two. We need to tell this story in full, and we need to see both sides of the question.

Telling Your Story

When we try to understand our identity, we can't just point at one thing to define ourselves. We are far more than any one part of our lives. When we try to limit our identity to one part of life, we aren't being honest with ourselves. We're missing something fundamental if we say that half of our waking hours don't count.

Both approaches above tried to solve the problem of the two selves by focusing on "real life," whether that's work or leisure. But regardless of which side, both approaches made the same mistake: they looked at work as something that exists independently of the rest of life. Each tried to understand work as something standing on its own and justifying itself instead of trying to understand it *in context*. This mistake leads to a vision of work that can only be purposeless. We need to look at work in the context of life to understand why it's meaningful.

We naturally understand things through narratives. We think about the world as a long list of connected stories. Everything comes together in these events chained one after the other, all with a clear thread linking them. When we understand our lives through this divided mentality of the two selves, we lose this unified life story. Instead, we are playing two different characters. Everything becomes disconnected.

When we are looking for a way to unite our work self and our home self, we need to find a common thread. We need to learn what story we're telling with our lives and find a way to combine everything into a clear narrative.

To answer this question, we want to know what creates real unity between work and life. What makes work dignified and worthwhile? What gives work a real sense of pride and satisfaction? Where does work fit in with the rest of your identity and with each part of your life? How can we find real *freedom* in work and life?

Throughout this book, we'll try to answer each of these questions in pursuit of happiness, fulfillment, and freedom at work. Taken together, we hope to use these to understand what transforms work into a *vocation*, something that truly completes your place in the world.

Now, what's our method for asking this question? What approach can we use to make these concepts clear?

A Philosophical Approach

In looking at these problems, we want to take a philosophical approach. Applying principles of logic to investigate these questions, we hope to arrive at an answer through reason instead of just through observation. What does this method look like? How can we seek a philosophical answer?

Plato, likely the most influential philosopher in history, presented all of his works in the form of a dialogue. Most often, it would be his teacher Socrates debating someone on a particular question. Each character would represent a different position on the problem, while Socrates would offer challenges to these positions. He would start by considering the assumptions most people would make on the problem then pose a challenge to it. Eventually, the debaters would find a new answer to the problem, then repeat the process to find another answer.

Through this long process of challenges, arguments, and inquiries, the debaters would eventually reach the true position. (Or, sometimes, they would learn that there is no clear answer.) It allowed them to consider all the possibilities before deciding what to believe.

This method is still used in philosophy to this day (though most often without the characters). Beginning with an assumption, offering challenges, and emerging with a new answer is a time-tested method to deal with difficult philosophical problems.

Just as importantly, it's also an excellent method of teaching philosophy. Using the Socratic approach doesn't just create an answer at the end. It shows how to work to the answer independently. It's not just meant to tell you what's right: it's meant to show you that you're capable of finding the right answer on your own.

This will be our main tool for approaching these questions: we'll begin with a common assumption, challenge it, and work to find a new answer until we've arrived at the true position. Through this, we can make a broad survey of the most important facts about each question.

To begin, we need to understand what work *is*. These struggles with meaningless work began with misunderstandings of work's place in life. We need to build an understanding of work that escapes these misconceptions. Vocation demands that we bring together everything in our lives, not just the parts that seem most convenient. With that in mind, what does a real understanding of work look like?

CHAPTER SUMMARY:

- Unhappiness at work starts when our working lives and our home lives feel split into two directions. We don't feel as though they pursue the same goal and we feel like we're not using ourselves fully at either.

- When we see these problems, we're forced to find an answer to move forward. But too often, our answer is just choosing one part of life to be the "real" self and making the other less important. This doesn't fix the division.

- To solve this, we'll take a philosophical approach to the problems surrounding work, looking for our assumptions and challenging them to find new answers.

REFLECTION QUESTIONS:

- What values do you see as most important for your working life? Think about your goals and principles. List some here.

- Think about the same question for your personal life. What are the most important values here? List some here.

- What do these lists have in common? What are the differences?

Chapter 2

Why We Work

Where does work fit into life?

The problems we discussed in the last chapter all started with mistakes about work: both thought of work as something separate from the rest of life. Under the punch-out and grind mentalities, we were left without a shared direction. They reduce work to something isolated and directionless.

If we want to tie together a full life story, we need to start by finding how these parts of life fit together. We now understand that work is not meant to be something separate from the rest of our lives, but where and how should it fit in? Is it something that just fills our days and accommodates the rest of our lives, or is it something more fundamental?

To approach this problem, we want to focus on work. Our goal is to determine what work is and what role it plays in a fulfilling life. Is it limited to one part of ourselves, or is it something larger? To start, we will need to develop a basic understanding of the definition of work, the reasons why we work, and how we connect work to the rest of life.

A Simple Understanding

We established earlier that we want to look at these problems through a dialogue between different ideas. Starting with our basic assumptions, we want to offer challenges to our ideas and emerge with a new perspective. Through this process, we can take a wide perspective on a question and think about all the most important factors.

Let's begin with the simplest definitions of work. What are the first things that come to mind, and what are the challenges to them?

At its most basic, we think of work as the things we do to support ourselves. We clock our hours and make our commutes because it's a means of keeping afloat. But even beyond our careers, we can think of other necessary activities as work: housework, for example, is needed for survival just like your career.

Looking at this, we could make a very simple division: work is just the things that you do out of some kind of obligation. You go to your job because you have to, you clean your apartment because it's necessary, a teenager gets a summer job because that's the only way to save a few dollars—in each of these cases, there's a feeling that you *have* to do this.

But this narrow definition seems to fall short. Plenty of people work with a sense of passion and enjoyment, not just out of obligation. We often hear the phrase "find a job you love and you'll never work a day in your life." It seems to imply that how we "feel" about our careers can turn work into something else: if you enjoy it, it's not really work. But a passion for work doesn't make it into something else. And often, work can feel worthwhile and satisfying even if it's difficult and frustrating.

Connecting work with feelings can be misleading. It puts the focus on its moment-to-moment existence. But we don't just want this surface-level perspective. We want to find the real meaning of work. It's clear that there's not one feeling that all work creates or one way that a person has to approach work. What do all these examples of work have in common?

Our first definition of work was a way to support yourself. Let's think about this for a moment: what sort of trait is this describing in work? This is describing the *purpose* of work. Is there a way to find a general purpose for all work? Let's look at a classical idea from philosophy: the concept of *teleology*.

The Study of Teleology

From a modern perspective, we rarely look at anything as inherently purposeful. We're likely to see purpose as something subjective or impossible to prove. From a scientific perspective, it's possible to see the world as basically meaningless: we think of everything we see as a long series of causes, like dominos falling after each other. Rain happens because certain laws in nature make water molecules behave in a certain way. A squirrel pursues food because it's following its instincts.

But for many thinkers in history, looking at the world purposefully was the *only* way to make sense of things. They argued that we can't understand why animals live in a certain way, why the laws of nature exist, or why humans behave as we do without thinking about what these things are directed towards.

These scientists and philosophers (for many, science and philosophy were the same thing) didn't think all these things were just the consequences of earlier events. Instead, they believed these things were aimed towards a particular end. We can't understand animals and plants by looking at the past. Instead, we understand them by looking at the *future*. These events in nature are directed towards a certain purpose. An acorn doesn't grow into a tree just because of a long series of causes beforehand, but instead because it has the potential to become a tree.

Understanding something by looking at its purpose is called *teleology*. To understand a thing, we can't just look at its past or present. Instead, we need to look at what it's directed towards. We don't understand the acorn until we understand the tree it will grow into.

For another example, think about how you understand a tool. Imagine trying to describe a screwdriver: you could tell someone that it's made of steel, its handle is rubber, it has a certain shape, and so on. You could say all these different physical facts about it, but would this really be an explanation? No matter how much you describe it, nothing makes sense until you've answered one question: "What do you use it for?"

Taking a teleological approach means focusing purpose before anything else. To understand anything, you have to ask, "What's it for?" What's the purpose of a seed, an animal, or a natural law? Now, the natural world isn't the same as a tool, of course. But we can still recognize a sort of purpose to these things. An animal's life is lived in pursuit of goals of survival and living well. This is a kind of purpose.

Talking about nature this way might seem unusual. It may go against some of our modern instincts: it feels like we're treating these things like magic. But it doesn't have to mean this. All it means is that the world is more than just random. Things happen for a reason, whatever it may be.

It's clear at the very least that we have to understand human behavior with this idea of purpose in mind. If we try to understand work without thinking about the reason behind it, we're making the same mistake. People don't make choices for no reason—though, of course, we can make choices for bad reasons. We can talk about how it feels, how much time we spend doing it, or what most people do for work, but none of these things really answer our questions until we understand its motivation. What sort of end goal defines work?

Looking at things this way gives us a better idea of what makes work unique. When we looked at each of these examples of work, we always had an idea in mind and a means to bring it into reality. Work is goal oriented: there's a clear end in mind that it's trying to achieve.

In a certain way, all work is a two-step process: we decide on a goal then begin working to make it a reality. The thought behind it is just as important as the effort.

The sculptor Michelangelo famously said, "Every block of stone has a statue inside it and it is the task of the sculptor to discover it." When he worked, he recognized a possibility and offered his own strength and talent to make it real. All work does this in some way: we hope to move something from an idea to a real thing.

This is our definition of work: it means moving something from *potential* to *reality*. It means putting in the effort to bring about an end goal. In everything from your job to housework, there is this process of finding an idea and working to bring it into actuality.

It's also clear now what separates work from the rest of life, whether it's recreation or idleness. When watching TV or sitting on the porch, we don't have a particular conclusion in mind. When we work, we always have to have an idea of where we're going: there is an endpoint for each job. There's always a clear vision of success or failure for whatever work we do. Once we've achieved that success, the work is done.

There's no equivalent finish line when we're at rest. Is there an end to sitting on the porch when you've reached your goal and are satisfied to leave? It would seem ridiculous to just sit out on a cool summer evening for an hour and say at the end, "Well, I've accomplished what I wanted to do, and now I'm done with this."

In this case, work is a simple fact of everyday life. How could we avoid work if it's something as universal as this? We're imaginative beings with constant goals and aspirations. This isn't something that's limited to your career. At our jobs and in our everyday lives, we're always directed towards the future.

But work's value isn't just what it creates. Work is also valuable as a means of understanding ourselves. It becomes a reflection of who you are and offers a concrete way to learn the significance of your life. If we want to make work and identity fit together, the solution isn't to abandon it. We want to find a way to dig deeper into it.

Regardless of whether work is our main purpose in life, it is always a *part* of a purposeful life. But work needs more than just an end goal to be worthwhile. When we're asking about a career, what makes it good and dignified? How can it elevate a human life?

Dignified Work

Just about everyone has dealt with a job that made it hard to live happily. Maybe it was monotonous and dull. Maybe it took over the rest of your life, demanding all of your time and refusing to let you pursue other important goals. At worst, perhaps you've experienced a job that was actively degrading: maybe you weren't able to support yourself with your work or maybe you struggled with an unfair boss. Whatever the cause, we're all familiar with this feeling.

Simply, we'd call this work undignified. It makes us feel lesser. We have a need for respect and satisfaction in our work, no matter what we do. Just what is it that gives work this sense of dignity, or what is it that takes it away?

Likely, the first thing we'll think of is how others perceive our work. It's important to us that our work is respected by others. We want recognition. Our first idea of dignified work may be prestigious work. We might think of doctors, lawyers, and high-ranking businesspeople. In this case, we associate dignity with status.

But we shouldn't just think of arbitrary metrics of status or success. These subjective measures can just as easily be a path to unhappiness and misery. An investment banker who works 100-hour weeks might seem prestigious and respected, but it's clear that this kind of life is still painful and miserable—if this is "dignified" work, then dignity doesn't seem that important. Instead, we want to look at work that emphasizes real human dignity. Instead of looking at these standards of success or recognition, we want to look at what makes life worthwhile in the first place.

Often, we choose these metrics to make a goal more concrete. Setting a goal like "being happy" might be worthwhile, but it's hard to think of immediate steps to pursue this kind of large and indefinite goal. Instead, we break it down into clearer and simpler problems to solve: instead of saying that you want work that makes you happy, you might set goals like looking for work in a certain salary range or getting a particularly prestigious job.

If we're not careful, we can become so caught up in these small goals that we forget the original target. We didn't choose these goals for their own sake. Instead, they were stepping stones to a larger goal. When we lose sight of this, we get caught up in meaningless distractions and difficulties.

When thinking about dignified work, we need to ask ourselves what the ultimate goal is. There's one goal we all share: we're looking for work that creates happiness and fulfillment. We need to remain focused on this when we set our standards.

Looking at things this way, we'll likely think of work that we traditionally see as meaningful. We might imagine someone working for charity or someone who's made a passion into a career. In these cases, it's clear how their work contains human dignity: these workers are pursuing a fulfilling goal in every moment.

But is dignity *limited* to only this sort of work? It might be the case that this is the ideal kind of career, but it's not the only route to happiness or fulfillment. There's still something we can find even without this particular sort of fulfillment. When thinking of what makes a job dignified, we can't just take a narrow view that ignores a career's place within the context of life. What happens on the clock is important, but we're making a mistake if we just think of dignified work in this limited sense.

We started by asking where work fits into life. With that in mind, we need to take a broader view of what makes human life worthwhile. We need to think of work in the context of human *teleology*. What is it that we're directed towards, and how can work respond to this?

Now, human teleology isn't an easy thing to understand. It's easy to think of the purpose of a screwdriver or a seed, but human purpose is a different thing entirely. Freedom changes things: once you can choose what you want to pursue, there's not just one reason for living. Is there any way to think of this without just saying that it's subjective or impossible to know?

We can begin to understand this by looking at one idea: human need. What are the things that we need to live well? From the most basic to the most significant, what are the requirements for a fulfilled human life?

Human Need and Human Potential

Dignified work means fully recognizing the dignity of each person affected by this work. From basic needs to complete fulfillment, we want to see every piece of humanity respected and cared for.

We can think of simple needs: a living wage or respecting a worker's limitations are obvious. These are the most essential requirements for dignified work. They're the foundation that everything else builds upon.

But it's clear that these alone aren't enough. It's easy to think of undignified work that can pay the bills and put food on the table: if you're still disrespected, stressed, and missing the most meaningful parts of life, your work is missing something important regardless of the salary. We need something more than the basics.

In psychology, there's a popular concept of a hierarchy of needs. We prioritize the things most necessary for survival. But when we achieve that, it's not as though this is the end of our needs. In the classical version of the hierarchy created by Abraham Maslow, these needs are (from least to most important) survival, safety, belonging, respect, and at the top, "self-actualization"—the need for purpose.

Let's take a moment to look at each of these ideas in more depth. To start, we can look at survival and safety together. These are the most basic needs of all: we want to meet our essential needs for life and find the stability that lets us keep them. When you work to pay rent, afford groceries, and save up for the future, you're trying to meet these needs.

But once you've met these needs, what's next? You won't just decide that you have all that you want. The point of human life isn't just to survive. Beyond these basic needs, we're motivated to seek something much more significant.

The next level, *belonging*, comes from our tendency towards community as humans. Aristotle once defined humans as a "political animal." By this, he meant that we tend to come together in community by nature. It's clear that this is a key need for everyone: we want to know where we belong. We want a place in a community, a role in society, and a feeling that we are wanted.

Of course, we also want a place that's meaningful and well regarded. This brings us to the next need: *respect*. Whatever your place is in the world, it's important that it's one that's worthwhile. It's no use finding where you belong if it's somewhere that you don't want to be.

It's easiest to think of this as the need for others to respect our role: we want to know that others see what we do and appreciate it. But even more important is the need for *self*-respect. It's easy to ignore all the positive recognition you receive from others and find a way to put yourself down anyways. Lasting esteem doesn't come from others. It has to start within yourself.

The most important factor for achieving this kind of self-respect is finding meaning and purpose in your role in the world. This brings us to Maslow's final level: *self-actualization*. This is the very tip of the pyramid, the last thing that we need to achieve for a complete life. To put it briefly, it means finding purpose in your life: self-actualization comes when you recognize what your life is "meant for," whatever that means. It's at this point that you can see everything come together and complete that self-respect that you were searching for.

It's here that we can see work's place in life: work is our means of achieving each of these different levels of needs. Yes, work helps us achieve basic needs, but it also helps us strive for belonging, respect, and purpose. That's what it means to respect human need. This is the real meaning of dignity at work. We can only understand dignified work when we think about completing all of these needs.

In the same way that we apply teleology to work, we can apply it to all of human life. The best way to understand our lives isn't just looking backwards retrospectively. We aren't just defined by the things we've done. We're also defined by the future that we have. Just as it's impossible to understand an acorn without knowing that it's meant to grow into a tree, it's impossible to understand the meaning of your own life without thinking about the possibilities available to you.

We live and work with a future in mind—this is where we find direction.

Of course, a person's potential isn't quite as clear as an acorn's. We have an element of choice: there's not a single determined end in mind. Whether our goals and personalities are mostly nature or nurture, it's still clear that we can decide what we want to pursue.

But what happens when work fails to join in this pursuit? What happens when work loses this direction?

Work Without Direction

The author Franz Kafka is known for his stories about massive bureaucracy and pointless, monotonous work. Characters are forced to deal with inexplicable rules, contradictory standards, and nonsense systems as they try to navigate the modern world. Today, the term "Kafkaesque" is used to describe a maze of bureaucracy where work seems pointless and hard to understand.

His last novel, *The Castle*, tells the story of a surveyor who's summoned to a local castle by the town's ruler. When he arrives, he finds that the town is ruled by unseen bureaucrats who nobody seems to know. The surveyor finds that he has no way to do his job and can't even speak to the people who've hired him. Still, his whole life is uprooted and he's forced to stay in the town.

After all this, the surveyor learns he's been hired by mistake but still can't afford to leave the town. He came here thinking he had a purpose and a place yet found that this was a lie. Kafka died before finishing the novel, leaving the surveyor's fate unknown.

Kafka's writing paints a grim picture of work. He drew upon his own frustrations working in insurance to write stories where work seems pointless and machine-like. Sadly, it's all too common for people to identify with this same feeling of directionlessness. When we're small parts of a big machine, it's hard to know just where we fit.

It's easy to see how a job falls short when it fails to meet basic needs. But what about a job that misses these higher needs as well? We aren't content with just the bare minimum. We're meant to be part of something greater. We can't just ignore our need for purpose and fulfillment.

We work with a particular end in mind, whether it be a clean room or a nice shed in the yard. In all these cases, there is something that is lying at the end of our work that we're pursuing. For many kinds of work, that goal is something immediately apparent: it's very clear what the goal of building a shed is and how your efforts will help you complete that. But with other sorts of work, it's not so easy to recognize why you're doing what you're doing.

In these cases where there's not some quickly apparent concrete goal, it's likely that the aim of work is just a better life. We work because we have a vision of our best life and we think that we can get closer to that through our career, whether it's simply through the resources granted by work or by something else.

Still, it's hard to say motivated daily with a goal that's so broad. We want something real and tangible. We want to see that our work has an impact and a purpose instead of being removed from it. We struggle when we feel detached from this wider goal.

These goals removed from work are worthwhile, but it's still hard to get over this disconnect. Work shouldn't just be a time to turn off our brains and forget about what we're doing until it's finished. When work feels like eight hours of running in place, it's hard to feel like it's doing anything to help us reach these higher goals.

How, then, can we identify purpose within work itself? Where can we find daily fulfillment and growth that creates self-actualization in a fuller sense?

To understand this, we need to ask ourselves what gives work this inherent value. We can talk about work's place in relation to human need, but what offers an honest sense of pride in a day of hard work? What gives work this sense of direction and worth for its own sake?

CHAPTER SUMMARY:

- Work is our means of bringing ideas to reality. It's our means of impacting the world, transforming things into something new.

- In trying to understand work and fulfillment, we should take a teleological perspective. Understanding something teleologically means thinking about its purpose and final goal.

- Dignified work meets all human needs, from our basic needs for survival to our higher needs for belonging, respect, and purpose.

REFLECTION QUESTIONS:

- We talked about the idea of teleology: you can only understand an acorn when you know that it's meant to grow into a tree. Think about this idea in your own life. Do you see that same sort of teleology for yourself? Do you have an idea of the person you're meant to become?

- Think about your goals at work. Are these "stepping stones" to something greater? Is it clear why you're pursuing these goals?

- We listed five major needs: survival, security, belonging, respect, and self-actualization. How does work contribute to meeting these five needs? Which needs does it fail to meet?

Chapter 3

The Hidden Beauty of Work

What gives us a sense of pride in our work?

Dignified work answers human need and builds on human potential. This shouldn't be something rare or limited: it's something we can find in all work. Starting from these basic needs, work should help us in the pursuit of higher needs for purpose.

Of course, work is worthwhile just for the good it brings. Cleaning out a dirty basement might not be many people's idea of "dignified" or "purposeful" work, but it's still good and useful if it's to help a struggling family member get their home in order. When we have this good end in mind, these difficulties are easy to ignore.

But we can find fulfillment in work itself, not just in its impact. We can take meaningful pride in what we do, no matter what it is. There's something beautiful that we can appreciate in the work itself. We shouldn't just think of the final product. We should think of the process.

Think of carpentry. A carpenter, like anyone, works for a living—this is the same as any job. But is the wage the only thing that makes this work worthwhile? Beyond these basic needs, there's a clear sense of personal investment in their work. When skilled carpenters build something, they feel pride in the precision of their cuts and the skill needed to do this work well. Disregarding the wages and the pay, there's something that's worth pursuing and working for within this craft.

It's clear that this isn't exclusive to carpentry. The same thing could apply to just about any career: a manager might feel a sense of pride in the talent needed to motivate and organize workers. An accountant might take pleasure in skilled analysis. Even something like stocking shelves at a grocery store has a set of skills that are worthy of respect and appreciation. Only someone familiar with this work can really understand what makes this so special. When we can see these unique skills in each kind of work, we arrive at its inherent value.

Now, when we talk about this "beauty," what are we recognizing? What sort of good are we seeing when we look at this?

External and Internal Goods

What makes anything worth doing for its own sake? In work, we have an end goal in mind, not just the work itself. The point of spending an hour working on a car isn't just having fun working on it. It's to fix it and solve a problem.

But a closer look at this example should show that this is not entirely correct. It's easy to think of people who would do this work simply for fun. There are mechanics and hobbyists who love the craft even disregarding the need for this work. Yes, they still work with a certain end in mind, but there's something worthwhile in the work itself.

Does this mean that this work isn't done with the same purpose as other kinds of work, or that work can only be fulfilling when you ignore motivations like money? No—instead, this points towards a new kind of appreciation for work.

Let's use a young student as an example. What motivates her to study? Well, at first, she probably reads because her parents force her to. "You can't go outside until you do your homework," they might say. Perhaps they'll try to motivate her with a gift at the end. Maybe if she earns a good enough grade, her parents will take her to a movie or bring her out for ice cream.

For her, the value of studying is the benefit that comes at the end. We don't expect children to want to do math homework or memorize vocabulary because they think it's fun. Instead, we have to offer them a different motivation that's not a part of the activity itself.

But a student growing older might recognize that there's something more valuable than the reward at the end. The student from our example might learn to love reading. Likely, she'll still think about the benefits of studying: instead of time-out or ice cream, she'll grow to think about grades and college admissions. But there may come a point where she stops caring about the grade and starts loving her studies for their own sake.

Perhaps she has to read *The Great Gatsby* for class just to finish an essay. She's focused on finding quotes, identifying themes, and creating an essay. But soon, she'll recognize that there's something more valuable than the grade she'll get at the end. She becomes attached to the characters, appreciates the writing, and comes to love the book just because it's beautiful. Now, she doesn't need those outside benefits to motivate her reading. Without any grades or rewards, she wants to read for the sake of reading.

This story is common to all sorts of hobbies and passions: we start off motivated by some external benefit only to find ourselves drawn in by an appreciation for the activity itself. A young kid forced to play baseball might come to love the game. A teenager might find a summer job at a restaurant and learn to love cooking. Although we start doing these things for an external reason, we still find something worth appreciating for its own sake within.

The philosopher Alasdair MacIntyre argued that these two types of motivations are split between *internal* and *external* goods. The internal goods are things within the activity itself: the pride that you feel in a job well done, the joy that comes from passionate work, or the reward of seeing yourself improve.

External goods are things outside the scope of an activity that are used to motivate someone. Look at the rewards and punishments above: we could think of children being punished or rewarded to motivate them to do well in school or play a sport. We don't have to limit this to children, of course. A professional baseball player who's just in it for the money is also motivated by an external good: he's doing it for some reward at the end, not out of an appreciation for the game itself.

These rewards aren't a requirement for the activity. There's no reason why you need a reward or a punishment to play baseball. Beyond that, you don't need to understand anything about the activity to appreciate them. Whether you're a baseball expert or you've never picked up a bat in your life, $10,000,000 means the same thing.

But we're recognizing something different when we appreciate the things required for the activity. When we appreciate the skill it takes to hit a fastball or the talent needed to make a beautiful poem, we're seeing something unique to each activity. These are necessary parts of each of these crafts. The only way to appreciate them is through experience and understanding. These *internal* goods represent the inherent value of things. They are the reasons why we'd do something for its own sake.

MacIntyre argued that these internal goods are *virtues*. Virtues, he argues, represent excellence in a particular capacity. When we admire good writing, we're looking for the virtues of a good book: good prose, carefully planned plots, or compelling characters. When we admire good baseball, we admire another unique set of virtues: the quickness of a center fielder, the patience of a great batter, or the strong arm of a hard-throwing pitcher.

This same model can be applied to any practice we might have. Take management for example: we might think of skills like motivation, organization, delegation, and so on. All of these are virtues necessary for good management. A good manager could appreciate these for their own sake.

These virtues are present in any kind of work. Whether it's accounting, landscaping, stenography, or stocking grocery shelves, there's something unique and special in everything. If you see someone doing menial work that you've done before, you're likely to appreciate the unseen skill required for it. Once you've had a job in a restaurant, you'll never look at the waitstaff the same way again. But no matter how others perceive this work, there's still something beautiful within it.

When you stick with the same sort of work for a long enough time, you're certain to recognize this worth wherever it may be. Even something simple can become beautiful in its own way: mopping the floor can take an incredible sort of skill and someone who's spent time mopping could admire how much unseen effort goes into it. There's beauty unique to all work. It's beauty that you can only understand through a long life of learning.

Internal goods are particular to each activity, but external goods are common between all sorts of different things. Money is an obvious example of an external good: we work for pay without really thinking about the value of these skills or virtues. You don't need any appreciation of the virtues to appreciate this value.

However, this is not an either-or. We can appreciate the internal and external goods of work. The living that we earn from a job and the virtues that we find within work aren't opposed to each other, nor is work better without these external goods. Work's beauty and this usefulness should go hand in hand.

We've seen how work can be valuable for its own sake. We can take pride in all work even without its good consequences. But we also emphasized that work and life should be unified in their values. If we're looking for the inherent value of work, we should look for what values it shares with life as a whole, instead of looking at it as a separate thing.

We can use this definition of virtue for just about everything: it's a skill required to do well in a particular activity. It's easy to apply this model of virtue to everything that we do. There are virtues of skateboarding and virtues of engineering, all of which must be gained through practice and all of which we learn to appreciate through experience.

However, we tend to use the word "virtue" in a *moral* sense. When we talk about *the* virtues, we're likely referring to things like patience, kindness, or wisdom. We're not thinking of some particular practice or activity. We're thinking about life in general. Put simply, we're thinking about what is required to be a good human being.

When we put it this way, the analogy should be clear: in the same way that the virtues of work represent excellence in those practices, the moral virtues mean doing well in the skills that are natural to human life. These lead us to be better as friends, as parents, as siblings, or as members of a community. In the same way that an accountant needs a certain set of skills to work well, we need things like patience and kindness to do well in life.

When we talk about *the* virtues, we are talking about the things that are necessary to live a fulfilling life. We're asking about the most important capacities we have as humans— beyond that, we're asking what it means to do our best in these. What are the skills needed to live well?

The Virtues of Human Life

It's not hard to think of a few virtues. But it's hard to create a list of *the* virtues. We can think of so many different examples—patience, humility, discipline, and so on. It's hard to choose just one set of virtues.

But taking a closer look, we can see that many of them seem to fit together: patience, discipline, and humility all seem to be similar. Virtues like kindness, generosity, and honesty are closely linked. In all these cases, it seems like there's one virtue that unites them. We don't need to list all of the dozens of possible virtues we could imagine. Instead, we need to find the virtues that combine these.

There are four in particular that capture the wide range of possible virtues: *wisdom, courage, self-control*, and *justice*. Through all the different lists of virtues made in history, these four have stood the test of time. Looking at each of these virtues, we can identify the most important things needed to make the right choices in life.

Wisdom is the power to judge the right and wrong thing to do. It's often called the "mother of the virtues" since we need it to use any of the others. Courage, for example, is meaningless without wisdom: if you always rush in without thinking, you're going to act irresponsibly. Well-used courage means recognizing when you have to accept a risk and push forward regardless.

It's impossible to know the right direction to go if you don't know your way about. Wisdom lets you find your footing. It means knowing the world around you, the choices you can make, and the goals you should pursue. Wisdom sets the stage for living well.

With all this in mind, there are a few different parts of wisdom. Naturally, it requires some knowledge. You can't know your way without knowing a thing or two. But just knowing the facts isn't enough. Wisdom also requires experience. To really understand something, it's not enough to know about it. You need to encounter it in practice. If you want to learn to drive, you need to get behind the wheel.

Virtue is always a product of experience. We only know how to choose the right path through a life of learning and reflection. Of course, it takes humility to recognize your mistakes and change from them.

Wisdom means seeing things as they really are. Once we can see through the fog, we can start taking steps forward. It cuts through the uncertainty and lets us find the right choices.

But knowing what to do isn't enough. We need to put these principles into action. Here, we see the importance of *courage and self-control*. These two offer us the discipline to put the right path into practice.

Courage isn't hard for us to understand. It's one of the virtues we admire most: we're all compelled by stories of people taking great risks, whether it's leaping into a fire to save someone's life or taking a dangerous climb up a mountain simply to prove it's possible.

Looking at these stories, it seems like there's a simple way to define courage: it means fearlessness. Courage means taking risks without worrying about the consequences. The more you're willing to take risks, the more courageous you are.

But this doesn't capture the real virtue of courage. Courage doesn't mean taking these risks for the sake of taking them. Courage requires the wisdom to recognize when a risk is worth taking—otherwise, it's just recklessness. Someone driving 100 miles an hour down a busy road might be fearless, but nobody would say that this is a virtue. Really, it's only *because* we can experience fear that we can be courageous. Someone with no fear could never understand what it means to face them.

We encounter risk constantly in life. From small interactions to huge life-changing decisions, we're always faced with the prospect of failure. Wisdom can't force us to make the right choices. We need other virtues to put it into practice. Courage looks at these dangers and gives us the power to overcome them.

Self-control is similar. Through wisdom, we can recognize our bad behaviors and identify better replacements. These bad habits, the opposites of virtues, are *vices*. These might be things like cowardice, greed, or cruelty, leading us towards a dehumanizing path where we fail to live up to our potential. But much like courage, it's not enough to know that these things are wrong: plenty of people know very well that it's wrong to get angry for no reason or drink too much but do it anyways.

If courage lets us resist pain, then self-control lets us resist pleasure. It keeps us from falling into a cycle of listening to our emotions without listening to reason

Vices need to be tamed by self-control. This means learning to understand your emotions and taking control of how they affect your actions. Just like courage lets us move forward in the face of fear, self-control lets us move forward when vice tries to pull us in a different direction.

Many different virtues fall under self-control: patience, temperance, and modesty could all be considered forms of self-control. Staying calm when you're frustrated in traffic, keeping yourself from eating or drinking to excess, and stopping yourself from showing off are all clear examples of resisting a vice. Self-control lets you act out of reason instead of out of a burst of emotion.

But all these virtues are meaningless if we don't know what they're for. We need to know what makes our actions good and bad, not simply how to choose what we want to do.

This is where *justice* comes in. At its simplest, justice means knowing what everything and everyone is owed. It means recognizing the respect and help that other people are owed. It means knowing your responsibilities and what you can offer to others. It means knowing where you belong and how you're meant to fit in alongside everyone around you. Wisdom tells you how the world is and justice tells you how the world is supposed to be.

This is a broad virtue. Justice covers everything from telling the truth to caring for your family to treating others fairly as a leader. Even if we don't realize it, these questions are constantly pressing on us.

One of the most basic explanations of justice is that it means fairness: we should treat others with consistency, never giving someone less than they deserve or giving someone preferential treatment when it comes at another's expense. Justice is the virtue that lets us find a consistent way to treat others rightly.

But justice shouldn't prevent us from going beyond fairness. Charity might not be required simply as a consequence of fairness, but we'd certainly consider it something admirable and virtuous. In this sense, justice also means looking for what's best for everyone and asking how we can achieve it. Justice searches for an ideal world. It's the job of the other three virtues to find a path and follow it.

Justice offers both a principle to follow and a goal to pursue. It means treating others fairly and equally, but it also means thinking about the needs of others. Justice sets the destination and the rules for how to reach it.

While these virtues might seem good and worthwhile, there's still an important practical question: how can we apply these to work? We brought this up in the context of everyday careers, but how do these fit in? What do justice and courage have to do with meetings and spreadsheets? The virtues must be practical. The goal should be to use them as guides for action and as a means to understand the shared goals of work and life. But they might not seem like part of an everyday routine. Where do we encounter things like justice and courage in everyday life?

Recognizing Everyday Virtue

Some virtues might seem clear in the workplace: it's obvious how self-control and wisdom apply to work. Others might seem less apparent. How are we supposed to be courageous in an office? What does justice mean for an average employee?

Let's consider justice as an example. Charity might be an important aspect of justice, but how does it apply to work? For most of us, it might not seem like we have the resources to be generous. It's hard to think of what we have to give if we're not in a position of authority.

If we think of charity just in terms of giving money, then it's clear that many of us can't really be charitable at work, at least not significantly. But this is not the only way we can be charitable. We can offer our time. We can offer a chance to speak or a moment of listening. We're always dealing with these questions of what others deserve and what we can offer in the workplace—all of these are part of living justly.

Courage is very similar. We might think of courage as facing fears to confront great danger. But courage is also needed to stand up against the consensus. Courage is needed to speak up for the sake of a coworker. Courage is needed to say the truth when a lie might be more convenient.

All of these virtues still have their place at work, just as they have their place in any human practice. Anywhere we are meant to be ourselves, we are meant to be virtuous. That means that every part of our life is a path to virtue.

Seeing how virtue transforms based on your position should say one very important thing: you can only understand virtue once you understand your place in life. The way that you practice charity will be different based on other facts about yourself: generosity will look different for a young person who's not yet financially secure and an older professional with more to give. Courage will look different for a firefighter and for a consultant. Yet in all these cases, the virtues still remain. Even if they are not the same, they are still natural to all of us and essential to understanding what we are.

We can see a certain beauty in work when we look at it with this idea of virtue in mind. Yet it seems that virtue is different for each person's life: self-control doesn't mean exactly the same thing for two different people. If we want to understand the real meaning of these virtues, we have to understand how they change to fit each life. We must understand what determines *your story*.

CHAPTER SUMMARY:

- A sense of pride in work comes when we recognize the internal goods of a job. These are the skills of work that we understand through experience.

- All of these internal goods are a sort of virtue. They represent excellence in a particular skill that's needed to be the best you can be at this work.

- We can apply this same idea of virtue to life in general to recognize four fundamental virtues that we need to live well: wisdom, courage, self-control, and justice. Wisdom and justice are needed to learn what to do, while courage and self-control are needed to put these ideas into action.

REFLECTION QUESTIONS:

- What are the goods that motivate you at work? What are the external goods and what are the values in your work itself?

- Think about your own work. When looking at others in your field, what skills do you respect? What are the talents that you are most proud of in yourself?

- Now, think about the virtues that you see as most important in life, not just in work. What makes these virtues important for living well?

Chapter 4

The Three Factors of Identity

How can you understand your place
in the world?

Alasdair MacIntyre once said that you can only answer the question of what you're meant to do today once you recognize that you're a part of a story. Purpose and potential don't exist in a vacuum. There's not one "right way to live" that everyone's meant to follow. There are principles and rules that apply to every life, but these only make sense once you recognize where *you* belong.

The fundamental virtues—wisdom, courage, self-control, and justice—remain the same in every life. These are the basic capacities that we have as humans. Yet it's clear that each person is called to use them in a different way. The wisdom needed to be a good manager and the wisdom needed to be a good chef might have something in common, but they're not identical. A firefighter and a salesman will both need courage at different points in life, but a different kind of courage is needed for each life.

Virtue represents the skills required to live out your role in life. But no two people play the same role. With that in mind, the skills we each need in life differ as well. To understand the virtues that you need to gain, you need to understand *the person you need to be.*

Our next question is clear: what is it that defines a person? Our goal here is to find what aspects of life can explain who you need to be and how you need to live. If we take virtue as our goal, what shows us the meaning of virtue in each person's life?

How Do You Define Yourself?

We need to find something *unique* to each person. If we just look at general facts about human nature, we'll certainly learn important things about people in general. We'll find shared capacities and behaviors. We'll recognize the need for the fundamental virtues in every life. We'll see that a few things tend to give us a sense of purpose and direction, like truth or community. These tell us broad truths about humanity, but they don't give us enough guidance to understand each person individually.

This also means we can't define ourselves by comparison with others. Many people might try to use a sort of competition to prove their worth or define their identities: it's easy to look at life as yourself vs. everybody, much like the grind mentality. You're either ahead or behind, better or worse. This is a simple way to understand life.

But looking at your identity this way doesn't focus on who *you* are. It focuses on who you're *not*. Comparison drives us to see things in terms of what we lack and what we want. Instead of looking for something within yourself, you compare yourself against a measure that's outside of you.

Instead, we want to focus on what makes your life unique: things like your passions, abilities, or the communities you're a part of. When you're looking to understand your identity, what you're really looking for is an understanding of *your place in the world*. To find a real sense of fulfillment, we have to understand what gives us a sense of belonging and direction. We want to know what defines each person's identity.

Knowing these facts on their own isn't enough. It's important how we bring these things together. A few simple facts about you don't define who you are. Instead, what defines who you are must be the *story* that brings them together. The person that you were when you were ten and the person you are now are different in many ways. But they're linked together by a shared narrative. It's just as important to understand who you were and how you've changed as it is to understand who you are right now. We leave deep footprints as we're walking through life, and those marks still mean something long after we've gone past them.

How can we put this into practice? We want to find a few key things we can look at to understand a person's place in the world. Though there are thousands and thousands of questions we could ask to try to get to know a person, we want to focus on some of the most important parts of life to find out what sort of person each of us is meant to be. We want an understanding of human identity that's teleological and purposeful.

This understanding starts with the past, but it's oriented towards the future. We need to look at each part of a person's life, from the beginning to the time that's still to come. Taking this perspective of past, present, and future, we can look at three ideas: where you've come from, what you are today, and what you're directed towards. Together, these offer a vision of your story and what virtue means in your life. To help this process, we'll identify three major factors, each containing three traits.

What defines your past? We used the phrase *where you've come from*. In practice, this means all sorts of things: your home, your family, your friends, the country you come from, and so on. It's all the people and places that made you who you are. Above all, your past is understood by the relationships that have defined you. The people and communities you've been a part of are the most important part of understanding what's made you who you are today.

Here, we'll look at three ideas: community, history, and social style. We want to look at the people who have surrounded us, the wider story we're part of, and how we've learned to relate to others as a result.

With that in mind, we can move into the present. What should we look at to understand this part of life? Of course, the earlier factors still remain: where you've come from is still a big part of where you are. But one thing seems most important for understanding your present moment: your *why*. What is it that gets you out of bed in the morning? What do you want to do, and what are the most important goals in your life?

Together, these form your *motivations*. We'll look at three main factors here: responsibilities, aspirations, and our time at rest. Responsibilities create a sense of duty. These are the things we *must* do, whether it's an obligation to a person or a certain principle you feel you have to live by. Aspirations are the goals we're working towards. These are the ideas we have in mind as we work. This is what we hope to bring into reality.

Rest, the last of the three, might seem unrelated. What does this have to do with motivation? This seems to be simply the time we spend doing things without any direction in mind. How does anything really motivate this? However, as we'll see, rest means more than just doing nothing.

Lastly, we understand the future of our story through our *potential*. This shows us what you can become and what you should direct yourself towards. Remember that we're always oriented towards the future: no matter what, we're always moving forward.

What captures this potential? We can understand much of it through looking at our past and present: looking at the past, we can identify achievements that serve as milestones in our lives. In turn, these help to identify the next factor: the talents you have today. These are the things you are already capable of. Lastly, we can look at a person's capacities. We want to learn how we can grow, not just where we are now. What can show us this potential?

These ideas can't capture everything about you. There's not a quick way to learn everything about who you are. But looking at a few concrete examples, we can start to see the stories that each person is a part of and how these affect your place in life.

With that in mind, let's go in greater depth in each of these categories.

Relationships

There's a classic saying: "Judge a person by the company they keep." Though this is often used dismissively, it does point to a true idea: a person's identity is tied to the people around them. Your family, your friends, even people who you've hardly known—everyone around you played a role in creating who you are.

If we want to understand life as a story, we need to recognize these other characters, too. Life doesn't make any sense if we try to understand ourselves without these people around us. Nobody is truly alone—in some way or another, we've all been defined by all the different people we've come in contact with.

These relationships represent *community*. These are the people who've had the most direct influence on us. It's hard to make any sense of ourselves without the context of those around us.

This affects every part of your identity: the way you speak, the goals you set, the work you admire—all of this only makes sense when you think of the people who surround you. To talk about your life story, we need to start here to make sense of everything that comes afterwards.

It's obvious how close friends and family influence your identity. However, this extends far beyond these immediate relationships. These are the most important people for understanding who you are, but it's clear that we're part of something even larger. For one, we might think beyond individual relationships and towards larger groups that we are a part of. Though these communities might not strike us as a relationship, there's still a similarity: we are somehow defined by this group that we're part of.

Think of the city you're from or the country you live in. Aren't these a part of who you are? We are part of these communities—and, in some way, they are part of us. If you were born in a different city or a different country, you might be a fundamentally different person. Even if it's not clear just how these communities have influenced you, they've still had a profound impact on the person you've become.

Many of the relationships that define us are only indirect. Though you might not have met your great-great-grandmother, she still plays a part in your life story. Though you might not have met the founders of your city, you wouldn't be the same person you are if they hadn't chosen this place to settle.

This is the factor of *history*. Each of us is part of a story much bigger than any one person. Your own life fits into a much wider story, one that gives context to the life you live now.

Isaac Newton is renowned for revolutionizing science. However, when asked about his work, he said, "If I have seen further, it is by standing on the shoulders of giants." Everything he accomplished was building on something that came before him. Although he was brilliant on his own, his accomplishments were only possible within the history he came from.

In the same way, your identity is built on a long history of other people. The old saying "it takes a village to raise a child" might be selling it short: It took a whole history to create the person you are today.

And, of course, this changes how you interact with the people around you as well. Though some of your *social style* might be so natural to you that it almost seems automatic, much of it is also a result of the life you've come from and the people around you. Whether you're an introvert or an extrovert, cautious or bold, or more logical or emotional, it's almost certain that the way you interact with the world around you is influenced by what you've learned from others before you.

These traits show both how you've been impacted by those around you and how you relate to those around you today. Think about where you place yourself in your relationships with others—what is the role that you want to take? Do you tend to take the lead or patiently wait for others first? Are you one to push for your own viewpoint or are you willing to compromise?

The present doesn't replace the past. It builds upon it. If we want to understand where we are now, we have to keep in mind everything that's come before. These relationships and history continue to play a role in our lives forever.

And, as we'll see, they play an important part in understanding our motivations. Our past helps determine what will drive us in this present moment. Your responsibilities and passions began here, but they continue driving us each day.

Motivations

For many people, the defining question of life is this: why am I here? What am I meant to do? On one level, this is a difficult question that belongs to philosophy and might not have a single answer. Yet it's also an immediate and practical one. In a small way, we're answering this question with every choice we make. The very fact that you choose to get out of bed in the morning and do anything proves that you have some motivation in mind.

To make sense of your story, ask yourself: what drives you forward? What leads you to make the choices you make and choose the path you've chosen?

Perhaps the most important motivation we have is a sense of *responsibility*. We're constantly thinking about our duties and the things that we have to do. There's something we feel like we're meant to do at the moment. We feel as though our lives are needed for something. Where are you necessary? Who relies on you and how?

Although we might want to be part of something bigger, we don't need to find something huge to start understanding this. If you want to find a *why*, the best place to begin is asking where you stand today.

It's easy to recognize responsibilities big and small. We might think of the responsibilities you have towards family and friends. In small ways, so many people you encounter every day rely on you. Think about driving: when you're on the road, everyone around you needs you to drive safely. If you chose to ignore the law, how many lives would be in danger?

Here, we might think of broader values as well. If you value honesty, your decision to tell the truth is a sort of responsibility. You've chosen a rule and you believe you should stick to it. This is a genuine and meaningful form of responsibility.

For the most part, you'll find your responsibilities in your relationships. Yet we might find a sense of responsibility beyond this usual close sphere. We feel a certain kind of responsibility for the people we meet every day, even if it's only indirect. We feel a sense of responsibility for people in faraway countries. We feel a responsibility for the world in general.

Of course, work can offer a tremendous sense of responsibility as well. Ideally, work should offer a chance to join something larger than yourself and meet a real need. Dignified work should make you feel necessary.

Sometimes, we may feel a responsibility that is simply personal. You might feel an obligation to read or study for your own sake. Perhaps you want to exercise not just for fun or health but because you believe that it's how you should live. These might just be a form of habit, but they also represent a way in which we feel responsible to become a particular sort of person. There's an ideal within each of us that we hope to uphold and grow into.

Responsibility ranges from the smallest things like chores or habits to the highest principles that guide our lives. It's all of the different obligations we live out towards others, whether it's those closest to us, people we don't even know, or even ourselves.

And, importantly, our responsibilities always reflect what we're able to do. It's absurd to say that someone has a duty to do the impossible: if you're incapable of doing something, it can't be a duty. Just like achievements, responsibilities tell us something about our capabilities: what you take on as a duty shows you what you can do.

While this sense of duty is important, we don't just work because of some feeling that we have to. We work with a goal in mind and an idea of the future. We work with *aspirations* in mind. We always have an idea of what we want from work and from life. This keeps us looking towards the future and thinking about how we can change.

What are these aspirations? They might be anything from career goals to your hopes for retirement to the vacation you hope to take this summer. Broadly, these are just the things that we see ourselves moving towards through our work. They're the end goal of our everyday efforts.

We're naturally future-oriented people. Despite all of our attempts to "live in the moment," it's hard not to think about where we're headed and what we're hoping to achieve. Done well, this is not a bad thing. This simply means living with a clear sense of what our actions are building towards. We want a healthy sense of ambition. We need to think about what our actions are for without becoming obsessed and losing sight of where we are.

But it's not just these goals and duties that motivate us. Interestingly, we find great insight into our real motivations in the moments where we seem to have no goal in mind: within *rest*.

Most likely, our idea of resting will be some form of "doing nothing" (or at least nothing that takes effort): we think of getting home from work and throwing on the TV or scrolling online for a while with no real direction. Leisure is a break from the active life of work.

We might just look at leisure as something that serves work. We rest to recover and prepare ourselves for the next day. Our rest is just the bare minimum necessary to keep working effectively. When we look at things this way, everything in life starts to revolve around work. It's a strange loop: we work to earn time to rest, then we rest to prepare for work. None of it seems to point towards anything greater.

But rest isn't just idleness. This time away from work doesn't just mean sitting and doing nothing. Think about the things you do to rest: maybe it's reading, watching sports, or gardening. Maybe it's listening to music or doing a puzzle. All of these can be restful, but all involve doing something. It's not just about avoiding work.

Instead, rest is about choosing things for their own sake. Work always means working towards a particular goal. Rest means working without this kind of goal in mind. This time offers a unique kind of freedom. When you have nothing else to do, what will you choose? It's in these moments when we get to decide what we want to choose without any restrictions. We have full control over what we want.

Once you realize what really drives you and motivates you, everything else seems to fall into place. Something as simple as learning an instrument or picking up a habit of running can change the way you see yourself and your abilities. Good rest lets us realize what we're capable of and put it into practice. It helps us learn what we want from life and what we're meant to spend our time on.

These motivations speak to what drives us. But they also begin to show us what we're capable of. Looking at the things that lead us to act in everyday life, we can see all the different things we're able to do. It's here that we begin to see who we can become. We begin to step into the future and look at our potential.

Potential

Each of these aspects of identity was meant to direct us towards what we can become. A good story always foreshadows its future. We can find clues of what's to come in each moment. With that in mind, what defines our potential? What shows us what we're able to become and what we should become?

Really, this is a teleological question. We're asking what each person is directed towards and what we're growing towards. What's the simplest way to understand something's purpose? When we're trying to figure out just what the purpose of a thing is, we're likely to ask one thing first: what does it do? When we're trying to understand how a tool works, we'll ask just what it does. When we want to understand an animal, we'll ask how it lives.

In the same way, it's natural to try to understand a person in light of what they've done. If you were asked to explain a little bit about yourself, you'd likely start with what you've done: you might talk about your job or your hobbies.

We define ourselves by our *achievements*. When we look at our past, we're likely to see our major achievements as landmarks to orient everything around. Graduating from college is a major landmark that separates your life into a *before* and *after*. Winning an award for your work could be another landmark like this. If we understand our life stories as past, present, and future, these landmark moments will define our past. We want to have these clear places in our stories that show just what we've done.

There are many different kinds of achievements, of course. Milestones in education and work might be the most significant for most people, but they're far from the only ones. Personal goals also define our story: for a woman with a passion for running, her first complete marathon might be a defining landmark in her life story. For a man with a passion for guitar, he might remember learning his first song as a major moment.

Often, the most defining achievements in our lives come when we have the biggest impact on others. For parents, there's no greater achievement than seeing their children do well in life. You might think of the people you've helped when you think of your life's greatest achievements.

But really, the achievements that seem the most important will differ for each person. What you see as the greatest moments in life might be hard for others to understand. For a baseball card collector, finding an incredibly rare piece of memorabilia might be a defining memory looking in the past. Someone without any passion for collecting likely couldn't understand this at all. These landmark moments help illustrate what's most important in our lives. They serve as reminders of what's most important to us. Looking at what really stands out in your past can make your real priorities clear. If while looking at your past, you find it easy to remember your achievements at work, it's clear that it's made itself a meaningful part of your life: it has become something you can use to understand your past and help tell your story. If it's hard to find these sorts of landmarks, it might be a sign that this unity is missing. These moments don't seem important to who you are.

These achievements also serve as signs of your *talents*. Unsurprisingly, what you've done makes it clear what you're good at. We gain confidence in our abilities by looking at what we've achieved already.

Often, talent seems like something you're simply born with. Some people with a lifelong affinity for something like math, science, or leadership seem like they were born to do this. Regardless of whether or not this is true, it's clear that there's some part of talent that seems beyond our control— in some way, it's natural.

Finding your talents can be a simple process: simply follow your passions and achievements and you'll likely find something you have the gifts for. When your motivations and your achievements overlap, you've likely found what your talents are.

It's important to look at this with a sense of humility as well. Humility shouldn't just mean selling yourself short, however. It should mean seeing yourself for what you really are. It means looking at yourself and recognizing your talents just as honestly as you could recognize them in anyone else. It's the ability to step outside yourself and look at who you are without any bias.

If you're not honest with yourself, you'll be left with a made-up image of who you are. Importantly, you'll miss out on recognizing the last piece of potential: your *capacities*. This is the growth that you're capable of. Though you might not have them now, in time, you could make them all a reality.

We can recognize this capacity much in the same way we recognize our talents. There will be flashes of this throughout our lives. Looking back and seeing a moment where you fell short, you can see just how you could grow to correct that in the future.

The most important capacities are the fundamental virtues. These are shared by all people by human nature: these virtues guide us in the most basic parts of human life, things like reasoning, putting our choices into action, and learning what's right. These all point towards the person we can develop into and the life we can fulfill.

But there's also something deeply personal within your capacities. It means growing to be someone who meets the expectations of all these earlier factors. Within your relationships, you find the capacity to be a good friend, neighbor, or member of the community. In your social style, you see a person who faces the world in a unique way. In your motivations, you see these things that drive you to get up in the morning and that lead you towards the future. These pursuits offer a picture of a person who's able to achieve these goals and reach the goals that your life is directed towards.

And, within your talents, you find the abilities necessary to live this out. All of these should come together without contradictions: you can find a path that unites who you are, what you want, and what you're capable of into one life of virtue and fulfillment.

What is your ultimate capacity? It means being a person who can live out all these different aspects of identity well: living up to the expectations set on you by your community and your history, achieving those things that formed your motivations, and maximizing your talents to become the best you can be at what you do.

Playing Your Role

Living out your potential means learning who you're meant to be and finding the virtues to live that way. Informed by your past, present, and future, you can find a path that gives you the talents to pursue the best things in life. This is how you're meant to live: as someone who brings all of these different parts of identity together in one unified life.

How, then, should we interpret the virtues in each person's life? In thinking about your life story, you need to ask yourself what kind of person you need to be to live out this role well. Looking at your community, your responsibilities, your talents, and so on, ask yourself: what sort of person does this ask me to be? What sort of person is needed to do well in all these different pursuits in my life?

For someone whose life story is defined by strong roots in a community, virtues of stability will be more important: this sort of person must be reliable, agreeable, and patient. Someone lacking these roots may need to find virtues of adventurousness: wise risk-taking, adaptability, and boldness will be more important in this kind of life.

In each of these cases, the fundamental virtues are still reflected: wisdom, courage, discipline, and justice are equally important. But they take different forms. Sometimes, living virtuously means being the person willing to risk everything for your goal. Sometimes, it means sacrificing for the sake of your community.

Always, virtue means living up to your place in life. You have a story and you have a role to play. It's no coincidence that we often try to understand our most difficult questions by telling stories. As humans, we want to understand things as narratives, tying different events together into one long story with a beginning, middle, and end. Understanding your own life is no different. The person you're meant to become is the person who can complete this narrative that you've developed through your whole life.

At times, it's hard to understand the significance of this. It's easy to feel as though your purpose is small in the grand scheme of things. But no matter how big or small, there is a place for you in the world and a person you are meant to be.

Of course, our work should be part of this purposeful living as well. Even when work is idle, monotonous, or meaningless, we still think of it as something meant for a higher good. It's impossible to avoid this sense that it's made to be purposeful, even if it falls short.

In work, it's easy to apply this idea of living out a role. If you practice law, you *become* a lawyer. It's easy to think of your identity in these simple terms: you are just the work you do or some other social role. But, of course, this is not enough. You aren't just a worker, and you aren't just a friend or a member of a community or anything else like this. You are all these things together, and all of these are part of one story.

Understanding your life as a story doesn't just mean applying these principles to work. Your story doesn't just apply to one half of your life. These virtues and goals need to be part of a *complete* life, not just at work.

When we understand these principles in light of work and responsibility, how can we apply them to the rest of life as well? When we're away from work and no longer working towards a goal, what do these principles mean? To understand this, we need to take a look at an unexpected place to recognize these virtues: we need to look at those moments where we're doing nothing. We have to understand *virtuous leisure*.

CHAPTER SUMMARY:

- Living virtuously means something different in each person's life. We all have the same fundamental virtues, but we use them differently depending on what we're meant to do in life.

- We can look at a few key factors to understand a life story: relationships, motivations, and potential.

- From these, it's possible to recognize what each person is meant to become.

REFLECTION QUESTIONS:

Try to identify the key examples in your life for each of the factors in this chapter:

- Relationships—community, history, and social style

- Motivations—responsibilities, aspirations, and rest

- Potential—achievements, talents, and capacities

Chapter 5

Leisure and Life's Fundamental Goods

What can leisure teach us about the value of work?

There's a popular modern parable about work: a traveling businessman meets a fisherman lazing in his boat on a pier. The businessman asks why the fisherman wouldn't be out fishing while the weather's clear and there's good work to be done. But the fisherman says that he's already caught all he needs for the week and so he's taking a moment to just enjoy the sunshine and the breeze.

"Imagine how much more you'd make if you worked every day. You'd double or triple your revenue," the businessman says.

The fisherman agrees—"But," he asks, "what would I use that money for?"

The businessman tells him that he could begin reinvesting it. He could get a motorboat to go out further in the ocean, hire whole fleets of fishermen to work for him, buy all sorts of new technology to identify the perfect fishing spots—if he kept re-investing all of this money, he could be a very rich man.

When the businessman's finished his pitch, the fisherman asks, "And then what?" He'd have all of this wealth, but what's left to spend it on? The businessman tells him that when he has that much money, he could sit around all day and worry about nothing at all.

"But I'm already doing that," the fisherman says. The businessman walks off, frustrated and questioning his views.

It's easy to think of the fisherman as lazy and the businessman as hard working. If this were the case, the moral of the story would be not to work too hard: don't be like the businessman putting all this effort into your work. Instead, be like the fisherman who spends as little time working as he needs.

But a closer reading of the story shows this isn't the case. This fisherman isn't lazy at all. He's spending hard hours working at sea and only resting when he's back at shore. Why should we see it as lazy to work every bit that he needs and take time to truly appreciate his rest?

In a certain sense, we might call him unambitious: he has what he needs and doesn't want more. He's identified what he truly needs to be happy. He works hard, but he works with a concrete and humble goal in mind. When we look closely, we realize that he appreciates the meaning of his work better than the businessman.

This story shows us what work and rest really mean together. These aren't opposites or enemies. Instead, each serves to bring a greater sense of meaning to the other. Work is fulfilled when it leads to genuine restfulness.

When we think about finding a direction for life, we shouldn't just think of our work. We need to think of what it means to rest well as well. How should we spend this time away from work? How can this time lead to a greater sense of fulfillment at work? The answer to this lies in understanding *authentic leisure*.

The Purpose of Leisure

Understanding who you are offers a clear sense of purpose and direction: you can find a picture of the person you're meant to be and understand how to pursue virtue to achieve this. Work at its best is a path to growing in these virtues and becoming something greater.

We've talked about looking at work purposefully: we can understand work as a means to bring an idea to reality. But the purpose of human life isn't simply to work. The purpose of your life isn't to find somewhere to be productive and work as long as you can. If this were the case, we'd be complex machines. We're meant to take time to appreciate and understand life, not just to work. We're meant to rest and take in the world around us.

If life should be lived in pursuit of one goal, we can't simply apply a set of rules to work and be done with it. Virtue doesn't just apply to our work: it applies to our leisure too. Virtuous leisure might sound like a paradox or an absurd idea: if we see leisure as doing nothing, it seems hard to imagine how we could apply these habits. How can we understand leisure as something active and purposeful?

We're likely to think of leisure as just time to do nothing. It's our way of unwinding and getting away from the stress of life. From this perspective, leisure is aimless. If work is done for the sake of something else, then leisure isn't done for any particular purpose—we might say that we want to rest or that we want to enjoy ourselves, but the basic justification is the activity itself and not some end-goal that we have in mind. There's no "finish line" for leisure like there is with work.

If this is the case, what's the purpose of leisure? How does it offer us any way to get closer to fulfillment? Earlier, we saw the idea of avoiding rest to work more with the grind mentality—if leisure is aimless, isn't this approach correct?

If anything, it might seem like the point of leisure is to work more. We have to rest simply because we aren't capable of working more. It's the same as letting a tool rest because it's overheating or leaving your laptop while it's on the charger.

This calls to mind the idea of undignified work from earlier. Undignified work treats workers like machines. It only worries about their well-being when it's profitable. When we look at leisure this way, we're taking a sad view of the meaning of work. Treating leisure as rest for the sake of work might lead us to reduce workers to machines.

It's easy to see how work can overtake leisure as well. If you spend all your time away from work just thinking about work, are you really at rest? Is a businessman reading financial news every day of the week genuinely resting? When work dominates leisure, leisure seems to mean nothing.

This leaves us with two options: either leisure is just a matter of wasting time or it's all about getting back to work. Neither of these seem to offer the direction that we want. What can we do to escape this problem?

The philosopher Josef Pieper talked about this problem in his work *Leisure: The Basis of Culture*. Here, he tries to cast a new light on the idea of leisure. The culture of ancient Athens, he said, took a different perspective on things: we work for the sake of leisure. All work is done for the sake of rest, instead of the other way around. This understanding flips our view of work entirely on its head. What's the basis for this perspective?

In ancient Greek, Pieper says, the word for "work" translates to "not leisure." It's a straightforward way of defining it: we understand it in contrast to its opposite. But it says something very important about their view of work and leisure together: work is *meaningless* without leisure.

What does this mean? Does this bring us back to the punch-out mentality, where work is just something we have to do and life is really about the time you spend away from work?

We've already seen why this way of life falls short. Work has value in itself. There are opportunities in work that are not found anywhere else: through work, we can grow in virtue and come to appreciate the beauty within everything we do. Ignoring this means losing out on a key part of life's meaning: without any kind of work, it's easy for life to become directionless.

Perhaps the simplest solution is to treat leisure as a different kind of work. We can look at it as another productive activity. Perhaps leisure is a time to develop virtues the same way you would at work. You can devote yourself to learning golf the same way you try to learn how to write a better brief. We can apply the same logic to both of these parts of life. Wouldn't this offer a unified purpose for both?

While this might create a kind of unity, it comes at the cost of forgetting what leisure *really is*. Work has a certain conclusion in mind: there's a point when you're officially done with it. There's not the same sort of thing with leisure. We don't listen to music or play golf because of some goal we want to reach at the end. We do these things simply because we enjoy them. Treating them the same way that we treat work seems to miss out on an important part of what defines them.

Now, it's easy to think of some challenges to this. There's obviously a goal to golf: there's definite success and failure. It's not accurate to say that we do it with no goal in mind at all—a golfer without a purpose would just be hitting the ball around in random directions. A musician with no direction would just play random notes and chords.

But we can identify one difference between the goals of leisure and work: in leisure, these are *internal* goods. Yes, there's a goal to these things, but it's always a part of the activity. In a certain sense, we work to be finished with work: when you're digging a ditch, your only goal is to finish. When you're playing golf, the point is to enjoy it for as long as you can.

We shouldn't try to turn leisure into more work. Instead, we want to find leisure that cooperates with work. We want to learn how these two can come together with a common goal in mind without reducing either side. Treating leisure like another kind of work doesn't seem to solve this problem. Where can we find a common direction between them, one that makes both more dignified?

Leisure and Contemplation

In leisure, we're not just looking to achieve a certain goal or become better workers. The point isn't to make the moment useful. The real point is appreciating each moment to its fullest. But what does this mean for leisure? How can we describe it?

Just as much as leisure is about enjoying the moment, it's also about learning to recognize what makes these moments worthwhile. It's about paying attention to the good things that surround us and finding what makes life valuable. Leisure is where we learn to appreciate and understand the best things in life.

Josef Pieper argued that we can only understand this when we look at leisure for what it really is: a kind of *contemplation*. Real leisure always means reflecting on what is valuable for its own sake. We might think of leisure as the search for something really beautiful. Recognizing beauty often means finding something that overwhelms our judgement: it's the fact that we can't simply explain why it's worthwhile that makes it so compelling.

The pursuit of beauty means looking for things that defy simple definition. Beauty doesn't just mean that something's entertaining or useful. Beauty makes us ask what really motivates us to pursue anything.

Defining leisure in this way might change our view of what constitutes good leisure. Those aimless activities like binging TV or scrolling social media don't seem to fall under this definition. Neither really seems inherently good: these simply seem like ways to distract ourselves. They don't offer us anything more than some time to avoid thinking about things. If this is all we can aspire to with our leisure, what's the point of life away from work?

Reflecting on this might reveal some uncomfortable truths about your life: maybe you really do value idleness and distraction more than anything else. Maybe you struggle to find things that are worth pursuing for their own sake. If your leisure seems like a waste, it might be a sign that you don't have any sense of direction.

This might seem scary. At worst, it might seem like this shows that all we really want is distraction and idleness. Really, it points to a fear of living life while paying full attention to what's around us. This time spent in reflection can change us, and this change can be frightening. It's far easier to try to avoid thinking about real life than to spend any time in it. A moment of quiet might force us to see things in a new way, and a change of perspective can force us to act.

But we can also find clarity and reason for hope. Perhaps you'll realize that your ideal sort of leisure is spending time with friends and family. Maybe you'll think about spending time reading and studying. Maybe you'll just think of time spent in silence appreciating the day.

When we distract ourselves, we try to avoid thinking about life. We let our attention focus on something that takes all the hard work away. Distraction lets us stop thinking altogether. Contemplation means learning to focus on something fully. It means reflecting on what's worthwhile and what really motivates us. It uses leisure as a way to live in the world more fully.

Leisure isn't just idleness. It's where we find what really drives us. Its purpose is different from work, but it's still directed to pursuing fulfillment.

When we say that leisure has no finish line, that doesn't mean that there's no direction. Instead, it means that there's nothing needed for fulfillment beyond the activity itself. What's the "end goal" of spending time with your family or watching a beautiful sunset? Is there an ultimate goal to reading history books or studying nature? These things don't *need* an outside justification to be good. Instead, they aim at the good on their own.

Good leisure lets us appreciate life more fully. Where distraction leads us to think less about life, good leisure lets us live more intensely. We might think that lazily scrolling and spending time with friends are both a kind of escape. Both take us away from the stress of a daily routine. But good leisure isn't simply an escape. It doesn't stop us from thinking. It makes us think about exactly what makes this moment worthwhile.

Think about the great moments of rest and joy in your life. Whether it's a relaxing evening watching the sunset, watching a movie that fully draws you in, or spending a few hours with friends or family, you'll always find that it shows you something about what life is meant to be. It shows you the beauty that we can find everywhere.

Leisure, in this sense, is the pursuit of the quiet that lets us listen to the beauty of life. Work looks at a good goal and seeks a path to making it a reality. Leisure sits still and learns to appreciate those good things that work aims at. Without leisure, we couldn't understand what work is directed towards. We need these reflective moments to understand the goal of work.

We might say that leisure creates the map and work takes the steps. It's through contemplation and rest that we come to recognize what's really worth pursuing. We aren't born with some perfect picture of our values and goals in mind. This is something that can only be learned through experience and reflection. Without the quiet of leisure, we have no way to understand the value of work.

Now, this doesn't mean that all leisure needs to be quiet and slow. We can see how these ideas apply to reading or spending a night on the porch, but they can also apply to going to a concert, having a good conversation at a bar, enjoying a satisfying meal, or watching a football game. What's most important is that it doesn't serve as a distraction from life. Instead, it should lead to a deeper appreciation of everything around you.

What are the values that we recognize within leisure? What do they share that makes them worthwhile?

The Fundamental Goods

What do we choose to pursue in leisure? We can think of appreciating a beautiful view, spending time watching a documentary, or having a conversation with friends. All of these things seem worthwhile for their own sake. For each of them, we can think of all sorts of variations that have the same motivations. But what values do these things share?

Looking closely at all these activities at their best, we find a few basic themes repeating: ideas of *truth*, *beauty*, and *community*. Whenever we pay close attention to any of these worthwhile things in life, we'll find these values present.

In small ways, we're encouraged to pursue truth. Whenever you spend time pursuing curiosity, you're trying to get a fuller understanding of the world. We see the pursuit of beauty in nearly everything: everything from monotonous work to incredible art can be beautiful if we look at it the right way. And the need for community is obvious: we're constantly driven by a desire for belonging and a sense of duty towards those around us.

Why do we pursue these things? Perhaps because it's our nature. Because of our power of reasoning, we want to understand everything. We naturally tend towards community. And our desire for beauty is so hard to explain yet so essential. The Russian author Fyodor Dostoevsky once said, "Beauty will save the world." It's a saying that's hard to understand, yet it feels almost intuitively true. Though it's hard to see just why it's so significant, beauty still seems to guide us in everything it points to a certain order in the world that we want to pursue.

All of these values justify themselves. If we try to explain what makes them valuable, we find that there's no good way to explain it. We're oriented towards them by nature. It's just part of being human. These values are a teleological goal for everything we do. We're always hoping to find these in some way.

One more thing should be clear: these things aren't limited to our leisure time. Work, too, can be directed towards the pursuit of truth, beauty, or community. These same values guide us in every part of life.

It's through understanding these things that we come to a full appreciation of work's value. We can't understand the virtues and values of work just by intuition or observation. It's important that we have this experience, but it's through contemplation that we can recognize what makes it worthwhile. Think about your own work: it's rare that you think in the middle of a stressful and busy day about how proud you are of your work. There might be a feeling of satisfaction, but it's hard to pin down. Often, it's only when you find a peaceful moment to reflect that you can start to appreciate this. In a quiet moment, it's easier to see the skill it takes to do your work or the real value it points towards.

Here, we start to recognize what work is capable of. We need this time spent alone with our thoughts to really begin to understand work's creative power and its purposeful direction. Work and leisure don't stand at odds. Good leisure recognizes the values that make work worth pursuing, and good work fulfills these values.

When we have something to devote ourselves to, it's much easier to understand what we're capable of. Leisure creates confidence that we carry into the workplace and into the rest of our lives. We should never lose sight of the value of good rest.

In leisure, we develop a new sense of individuality. For as important as work is in nearly everyone's life, it's often hard to understand someone's personality through work. However, when we have this opportunity to pursue things out of an honest passion, we see much more clearly just what makes each person unique.

Losing leisure does not just mean losing out on something enjoyable or restful. It means losing one of our greatest opportunities to become who we are. In creative and active leisure, we see ourselves living fully: in a small way, we all have a chance to look for what makes life worth living.

Work and leisure don't stand at odds. Instead, they work together. Each is done in pursuit of the same values. Each is a path to virtue and fulfilling our human potential.

This potential comes together when we have a chance to choose a goal and pursue it independently. We find fulfillment when we can find the right things to pursue and choose them independently. Looking at this, we see the most important human capacity: *freedom*. Through virtue and contemplation, we can find a vision of what it means to truly take control of your actions and live freely. Real freedom fulfills this pursuit of virtue. Now, what does it mean to exercise this freedom to its fullest?

CHAPTER SUMMARY:

- We need to learn to apply virtue to every part of life, even when we are at rest.

- Leisure isn't just idleness. It's the time that we spend focused on values like truth, beauty, and community that are worthwhile on their own.

- Good leisure is also a time for contemplation. At its best, leisure should tell us what makes work worthwhile and motivate us in the pursuit of good things everywhere in life.

REFLECTION QUESTIONS:

- Think about how you normally relax. Does your relaxation feel like a way to "escape" from life or a way to live life more fully?

- Can you recognize similar values between your work and leisure? Do the things that make rest good also make work good?

- What does "contemplation" mean for your life? Where do you have an opportunity to reflect on the meaning and purpose behind each part of your life?

Chapter 6

Freedom and Choosing Your Rule for Life

What does it mean to live freely?

When Henry David Thoreau was 28, he decided to make a radical change. He gave up his old comfortable lifestyle, built a small house in the woods, and lived there for the next two years. He spent most of that time alone. Much of it was spent learning independence and self-sufficiency: he learned to farm, forage, and live a life of self-reliance. The rest of his time was spent in contemplation, thinking about what all this meant.

To explain why he made this change, Thoreau wrote, "I went to the woods because I wished to live *deliberately*." He said that many people seem to live life passively: though they may be unhappy or dissatisfied, they are too afraid to make a change.

He hoped that taking a radical step would let him escape from the "quiet desperation" he saw others living through. Everyone around him seemed to want something more, yet nobody seemed able to go out and find it. Escaping into the woods was his attempt to take control and make a change.

Though Thoreau made his trip to the woods all the way back in 1845, his story still resonates with us today. His fear of passive living and unfreedom feels relevant no matter the era. Many people still dream of following Thoreau's path and making a radical change, choosing a life that breaks away from expectations in search or something different.

The idea of a life lived *deliberately* appeals to something deep within each of us.

This freedom that Thoreau wanted is the real goal of our pursuit of virtue. Using your reason to make your own choices is *real* freedom and the final fulfillment of the pursuit of virtue. This is the goal we're after.

Freedom and Virtue

We looked at four major virtues that define our capacities as humans: wisdom, courage, self-control, and justice. These are the skills needed to live human life well. But we aren't simply reducible to these four things. Together, they're meant to build to something greater.

What do these virtues do for us? Looking closely, one theme becomes clear: each of them deals with *making choices*. Wisdom means knowing your way about and understanding how to pursue your goals. Justice means judging the right order of things, asking what we owe to others and what's right for each person. Courage and self-control help us take command of our actions instead of letting ourselves fall under the control of something else. Cowardice really means obedience to fear instead of reason, and vices like gluttony mean obedience to wants.

Now, we see just what these virtues mean in practice: *freedom*. It's our ability to make these choices on our own that sets us apart. We have the power to decide what we want and how we will pursue it: this is the real good that we hope to find through virtue.

Freedom means making choices based on your own power of reason. We need the virtues to give us self-control and understanding. Without wisdom and justice, we don't know what's right to pursue or how we should achieve it. Without courage and self-control, we won't have the power to overcome obstacles and put these virtues into action. When we say that someone is acting irrationally, we're saying that they're acting without real freedom in a certain sense: there's either a lack of understanding or a lack of control.

It's this freedom that makes humans unique. It's what lets us live purposefully. If life were simply a matter of following instructions, the meaning behind our actions would disappear. Our lives are meaningful because we aren't set on a single straight path with one answer. We're left to ask ourselves what a real answer would be and how we could pursue it. Fulfillment comes from choosing something meaningful yourself.

Looking at this goal of living freely can get us to the root of our wider questions for work. We found that many of the problems we face start with a feeling of disunity. There's a lack of integration between how we live at work and how we live the rest of our lives.

At its core, this means that there's a lack of freedom. A lack of integration begins when you feel as though you're making choices against your will. For some reason or another, it's as though you're forced to do something rather than choosing it. There may be a sense that you're failing to live the way you should: though you believe you're meant to follow one path, you choose another because you lack control. The choices you make seem limited somehow.

In everything that we pursue, we want to know that we're acting based on what we want and not following some rule we didn't choose. Our next step, then, is to ask what it means to make these choices in work and life. What lets us live freely in each part of life? What does it mean to make a real free choice?

The Meaning of Freedom

Freedom is what defines us as humans. Yet for as important as it is, it's difficult to nail down just what it is. What, then, is the real meaning of freedom?

The simplest idea of freedom might be living life without any rules or restrictions. We often think of freedom as simply doing what you want—in this case, living freely means acting with nothing holding you back. It means living without anything keeping you in check.

What does this mean in practice? The simplest interpretation might be a life lived for pleasure. You find the things you want and take them. It's the freedom to follow your basic instincts and desires without much of a second thought. Complete freedom would mean a direct path to whatever you want whenever you want it.

But what's the conclusion of living this way? Where are we led if we simply pursue whatever we want whenever we want it? Living this way is a kind of addiction. It means losing all control over your choices. Instead of acting out of reason, you act on momentary wants. This sort of compulsion isn't real freedom. This is a total lack of self-control—and this means that you can't make your own choices.

Instead of making rational choices, you're obeying a feeling. It's not something that's really in your control, and it's certainly not something that comes from your own reasoning. Addiction is perhaps the worst kind of unfreedom: you no longer have any power over yourself.

What would it mean to live without obeying anything? Really, we're always obeying something with our choices, whether it's a rule you're following or a want you're pursuing. The question is what we choose to obey. We could choose to listen to our instincts the same way an animal does, we could choose to accept a strict set of rules made by someone else to follow, or we could follow a method of reasoning that helps us find the answers independently.

It seems like the only way to live without this sort of obedience would be to live totally randomly, making decisions without any particular reason in mind. But this still isn't freedom. There's no control: you don't know the consequences of your actions or the reasons behind them.

No matter what, we can't escape these rules we live by. Strangely, it's here that we see the real meaning of our freedom. Freedom doesn't mean a life with no restrictions. Instead, freedom means *choosing* what rule to live by. We can choose what rules guide us through life. We aren't obliged to follow our instincts or to give up our freedom altogether. Through virtue, we are able to choose a different path.

Seeking freedom by escaping restrictions means looking for what we might call *freedom-from*. When we talk about freedom in this way, we're talking about removing the obstacles to freedom. Someone who wants to live with no obligations or rules is looking for a life of freedom *from* these impositions. It means getting rid of something.

But is freedom really just negative? From this perspective, it seems like all that it means to be free is to lack something. If we see freedom as something fundamental to the human person, this isn't enough. Humans aren't humans just because of something we don't have. Is there something you can take away from an animal that will give it the same kind of freedom a human has? Clearly not. Freedom must be something that we *have*. We need to find a *positive* freedom.

When we look at the idea of freedom-from, there's a natural opposite: *freedom-to*. Instead of thinking about freedom as something that tells us to avoid a certain kind of thing, we can think of freedom as offering an opportunity. Real freedom gives us something new.

When we looked at the factors of identity, what we were looking for was your place in the world. Understanding your story is the beginning of understanding the law for life that you want to live by: once you know your responsibilities, your goals, and your potential, you're offered a choice of what you want to become. Altogether, these show a range of choices that we could make. But this must be a free choice. If this choice were forced upon you, it would mean you're not using your power for freedom. Deciding who you want to be *must* be a free choice.

This is the most important choice that we make in life. When you choose who you want to be, you are choosing a rule to live by. We could call this an *ethic* for life as well. It means choosing a goal to follow and a set of principles to achieve it: *this* is the person you want to become, and *these* are the virtues needed to become that person.

An ethic for life means many different things. It means recognizing your duties: what are your responsibilities? What rules do you want to live by? Just as importantly, it means deciding what you value. What are the things that you see as worth pursuing in life? What makes life good, and how can you pursue that?

This is the real meaning of freedom: *deciding what to devote your life to*. At its best, freedom means making this deliberate choice to follow a path and pursue a goal. Understanding what defines you sets the stage for a real free choice made from reason.

In fact, it seems like nearly all our struggles with finding meaning and fulfillment return to a lack of freedom. When we don't have the power to make a free choice, it's hard to find anything fulfilling. We need this power of reason to make our actions feel purposeful. The pursuit of meaning means a pursuit of freedom, in life and work.

Freedom at Work

Freedom means making a rational choice about what rule you want to follow. In the end, we cannot live without some law: we always have a reason that's guiding us. This reason is a rule that we accept.

But although we're always using some sort of rule, there's nothing that requires us to use the same rule consistently. All of us can be hypocrites: even if we have a clear ethic for life in mind, we're not required to follow it. Without a doubt, we've all made choices that went against our principles, and we're all familiar with how painful it can be to reflect on these mistakes.

This hypocrisy is an obstacle to happiness and fulfillment. There's no worse feeling than feeling like you've betrayed your values. If you feel like you've failed to follow your chosen ethic, it's hard to get past the guilt.

When we feel a lack of integration between work and life, *this* is what we're feeling. It's a certain kind of hypocrisy: you feel like your life is based on two different ways of living. We feel pulled in two separate directions when it seems like we're living based on two different rules for life. When work and life each have separate goals, we're left without a shared ethic between each.

Our pursuit of unity between work and the rest of life is fulfilled by a real sense of *freedom*. Work and life can only be united towards one goal when you are free to choose what you want to pursue and how to pursue it. We don't stumble upon unity: it's found by intentional and reasoned choices. These are only possible through freedom and self-control.

Pursuing unity in life means pursuing freedom. But concretely, what does this mean in the workplace? What does work that values freedom look like?

Disunity at work is a kind of hypocrisy. This isn't just in the sense of saying one thing and doing another. It's also hypocrisy in the broader sense of living in a way that goes against your values. Prioritizing work over family can be a type of hypocrisy. Accepting a job that you don't feel capable of could be another type. If you feel like you have two different rules for life, it's hard for anything to seem purposeful.

Freedom is necessary for purpose and self-actualization at work. Really, freedom at work is just an extension of dignified work. We've already looked at the most important parts of dignified work: it's work that meets your needs and offers you an opportunity for growth. It's work that respects your humanity and offers a chance to develop it further.

Dignified work is a path to virtue. This means it should also be a path to freedom. The practice of virtue means making the right choices and putting them into action. Without the opportunity to make these choices, there's no way to grow. We need to practice to get better.

Often, we see these opportunities taken away in the workplace. Micromanagement removes the chance to grow and learn. Refusing to offer any freedom or flexibility for a worker to approach a problem can be an obstacle to dignified work. This might not be undignified in the usual sense: it's not the same as most degrading work. But it can show a lack of respect for a worker's dignity. Placing too little trust in workers is still degrading, even if it's only in a small way.

In thinking about the wider virtues of life, we shouldn't ignore the particular virtues of each profession. Mastering your work, whether it's management or craftsmanship or anything else, is an opportunity to recognize your own potential and the beauty of your efforts. If you're never challenged at work, there will never be an opportunity to grow in these skills.

Of course, the greatest obstacle to fulfillment at work comes when it seems like it has nothing to do with your goals in life or even goes against them. If you feel like your life is meant for one thing and your work is meant for another, your choices don't feel like they matter. What does free choice even mean if it only applies to part of your life? Freedom doesn't make sense without direction. Whenever we make choices based on reason, we're always making them with a goal in mind. It's impossible to make a choice with no reason in mind: though we might do things idly or thoughtlessly with no idea of why we're acting that way, all of our intentional choices must have some justification. Whether it's as simple as drinking because you're thirsty or as complicated as choosing a line of work because you believe it's fulfilling, we always have something we're aiming for.

Work that offers real freedom will offer an opportunity for unity. It will let you pursue your place in the world, growing in virtue and meeting the responsibilities that define where you belong. When we speak of work overwhelming the rest of life, it means that it sets a goal that stops you from reaching other important things. It stops you from living out the virtues or from fulfilling your responsibilities. How can you be the person you're meant to become if work goes against it?

Work that respects human freedom will naturally avoid this problem: dignified work allows you to set your goals for life and help you achieve them. Instead of an obstacle, it is an opportunity. Often, we may find that the obstacles in our work are self-imposed. When we prioritize success at work over all else, sacrifice in other parts of life to get ahead, or lose sight of work's importance as a path to other good things, we will find that we've lost direction elsewhere in life.

Whether your goals are centered around work, community, or something else, it's important that you choose something that can be a goal for *all* life, not just a part of it. We must find a consistent rule for life. This is the last key to fulfilling work, and the one that ties everything else together. Every idea that we've discussed so far builds up to work that offers an opportunity to live life based on this free and rational ethic for life.

After all this, we've seen what defines work that joins a fulfilling life: work that is purposeful, dignified, virtuous, free, and fits in your place in the world. Finding work that fits these criteria is a path to full integration and fulfillment. This should be our goal in discerning a path for life.

This kind of work is your *vocation*. This is the final step on our journey: beginning with everyday work, we've pursued a vision of something that offers a real opportunity for unity. Now, in defining vocation, the end of our search is in sight.

CHAPTER SUMMARY:

- Freedom isn't just the ability to live without restrictions or predictability. It means choosing the rules that we want to live by and deciding what we want to pursue.

- Real freedom comes from mastering the virtues and making choices from our own reasoning.

- Achieving real freedom is the solution to the problem of disunity between work and life. When we live intentionally based on our chosen goals, principles, and values, we can escape this feeling of separation and achieve real unity between each part of life.

REFLECTION QUESTIONS:

- Where can you recognize yourself living passively in your own life? Where do you find it hardest to take control of what you're doing?

- What would deliberate living look like in your life?

- Do you live by a consistent rule or ethic? What are the most important principles that you live by? Do you feel that these apply to each part of your life?

Chapter 7

Understanding Vocation

What sort of work should we strive for?

Many European monasteries of the Middle Ages lived by a simple guiding principle: *ora et labora*, or "work and prayer." Under this philosophy, each monastery chose a line of work and devoted themselves fully to it. Whether they were farming, copying books, or brewing beer, they brought all members of the monastery together to pursue one line of work and one unified goal.

This work was practical: it was how they made a living and supported themselves. But even though it was practical, it was also deeply contemplative. It became another way of reflecting on life's purpose. Work, as part of their routine, was a way of focusing on greater things. The quiet and consistency of this time allowed them to focus on life's final purpose and to recognize the value of their time.

In this life, work is a partner of contemplation. It's a means to balance life between practice and reflection. Even in those moments at work, life is directed towards something greater. Working the fields isn't just about the wheat you harvest for bread. It's tied in with reflection and meditation to create a life that is lived in constant pursuit of an ultimate end. Each moment comes together to form one rule for life, one person, and one goal.

Although this principle was invented for monasteries, it's clear how it can apply to our everyday lives. This rule offers a solution to the original problem we faced when we recognized a sense of division at the heart of unhappy work. When we've finally learned how to live this principle out in life, we've arrived at the solution to this problem. At last, we've arrived at *vocation*.

Defining Vocation

Vocation is the work that lets you live up to your place in the world. In the many misconceptions about work we've looked at so far, a job has been something separate from the rest of life. It's either its own world with a purpose separate from everything else or just a necessary evil that we can't avoid. In either case, it seemed to stand apart from who we are.

Yet neither of these ideas tell the full story. Work isn't the ultimate end of life and it isn't some sad imposition. Instead, it's a part of your life story and identity. Vocation doesn't mean finding work to live for. It means finding work that lets you live fully.

It's easy to think of work as either just a means or just an end. It's something that we dedicate our lives to or something that we only do in pursuit of something else. But neither of these approaches captures vocation. We don't pursue it only for its own sake. Like all work, it's done with a particular goal in mind beyond itself. If we think of the context of a life story, then we have to recognize vocation as a tool to achieve other ends in life: we work to support ourselves, fulfill our responsibilities, and build a complete life. We can't make sense of work while ignoring these goals.

When thinking about your vocation is, the question you need to ask isn't, "What do I want to do?" Before that, it's, "What do I want to be?" If you just try to look at work on its own, it's easy to get caught up in little likes or dislikes while losing sight of the greater picture. Vocation exists within a full life. A sound approach has to begin with this in mind.

But we can't make sense of work while ignoring the good inherent to it. Work may not be something that we pursue exclusively for its own sake, but it is something that's valuable on its own. In vocation, work is part of who you are.

Instead of thinking of work as either a means to an end or an end itself, we should think of it as part of something greater. Vocation begins when you recognize who you are and who you're meant to be, and it's fulfilled when you learn what kind of work fits into this vision. Through vocation, work becomes a tool to achieve this goal and become the person you aspire to be.

Finding your vocation means finding the work that you're meant to do. However, we shouldn't confuse this with an idea of destiny or fate. It's not as though every happy worker was chosen from birth for a certain career. Instead, it's a rational decision: by looking at the factors that make you who you are, you gain an understanding of the possibilities for your life. You learn who you want to be and where you belong.

This sense of belonging in your work is the core of vocation. Vocational work becomes both a practical tool for living up to your place in life and a source of purpose in its own right. This does not mean that your life *revolves* around work. It's work that becomes a seamless part of your life.

Baseball player Rogers Hornsby was once asked what he did when baseball season was over. "I'll tell you what I do," he said. "I stare out the window and wait for spring." In the end, nothing in his life had any clear meaning outside of baseball. When we think about vocation and pursuing purpose, we might want this kind of unlimited devotion.

We want to find something worth giving everything to. Our idea of purpose is a painter obsessively working all day, an athlete who never stops practicing, or someone who sacrifices everything to work for others.

But, as we'll find, life has plenty of winters. If we try to focus on one single thing as our unifying purpose in life, we'll lose sight of what makes other things meaningful. Even if springtime is the center of our lives, the winter is still a part of what we are. Focusing on just one part of this ignores a crucial part of who you are.

A life of vocation doesn't just mean giving more time and energy to your work. Certainly, this may be part of it: if you find a passion for your work, it's good to respond to that and develop it further. But vocation doesn't mean giving everything to work. It means your work giving you everything it can.

Defining vocation is one thing. But finding it is another. We know what we're looking for, but how can we find it? How can we identify work that's worthy of vocation?

The Four Principles of Vocation

Though we need to understand vocation as one part of a fulfilled life, we should keep in mind that it is still work. It means finding work that's part of life's larger direction. For all the philosophy and reflection surrounding it, we can't lose sight of the practical facts. Real vocation isn't just in your mind: it's something that you're living out each day.

We've spoken about understanding life's meaning through leisure and contemplation. It takes time and attention to recognize the value of work and your own life's purpose. But this doesn't mean that vocation is reducible to a change in your mindset. It's a concrete product of good work. Often, this does mean changing your approach to work. Still, there are important qualities a career must have to create a vocation. We need to learn to look for these qualities in work— either to recognize where they're already present, or to learn where to look for work with these qualities. As we've worked through these questions about work, meaning, and human nature, we've found a few qualities that are needed for vocational work. At each step, we've seen another trait of work that contributes to finding fulfillment. Throughout this search, we've found four particular qualities that are most important for vocation: dignity, virtue, identity, and freedom.

We've already spent some time discussing each of these concepts. We'll now look at each in the context of vocation to understand just what it means when applied to this part of life.

When we first began looking at the meaning of work, we arrived at the idea of *dignified work*. At its most basic, this means work that is made with the human person in mind. It's work that respects the needs and abilities of the worker and that offers an opportunity to grow into something greater.

In the context of vocation, we must also think of this as work that fits into a complete human life. Work's dignity goes beyond the time that we spend laboring. It's also about work's place in life. At its best, dignified work means the pursuit of self-actualization. It's meant to help you become the person you're meant to be. The basic needs that work responds to are important, but it's not enough to end with these. A person needs more than just survival.

How does your work serve that goal? How might it go against it? Work that demands too much will go against this pursuit. On the other hand, work that offers too little will feel insufficient. When we set aside a part of life for work, we hope to find work that fills that space fully—no more and no less.

Work finding its proper place in your life means fitting well alongside the rest of who you are, but it also means offering an opportunity for growth. Through the inherent goods of work—the *virtues* that offer meaningful pride in a job—we can find a means to grow in our natural capacities. In good, dignified work, we find something to value simply for its own sake.

This is what it means for work to fill its place in life fully. Work without this sense of inherent value doesn't feel worthy of the time we set aside for it. It becomes a monotonous drag and something that seems disconnected from the good that we pursue elsewhere. Without this idea of virtue in work, we can't find this same passion.

Perhaps the most important part of developing this passion is finding appropriate *freedom* at work. The fundamental virtues—self-control, courage, wisdom, and justice—find their fulfillment in free and rational choice. Without freedom, these are meaningless.

Freedom means knowledge and control: it's the power to know what you're doing and make a choice without anything impeding you. Work at its best should be both an opportunity for freedom and something chosen freely itself. Workers deserve the independence to make choices out of their own powers of reason in the workplace, not just following commands blindly.

For one, this means that the work itself should be freely chosen. Vocation can't be something forced upon you. This doesn't mean that your vocation has to be a dream job or that you can't make a decision out of necessity—working to pay the bills doesn't mean you don't have a vocation. However, it does mean that you must keep the opportunity to choose this work with a full understanding of what it is and full control of your choice.

Within the workplace, freedom means control over how you do your work. It means a chance to exercise the skills of work on your own, to act independently, and to take control of what you do. We shouldn't just be passive in work. Vocation means taking an active role.

All of these traits only make sense in light of your *identity*. To understand vocation, you must know what your story is and learn where it fits in. When we say that vocation is part of something greater, we're talking about a lifelong narrative that combines your past, present, and future.

We looked at this narrative in light of relationships, motivations, and potential. Vocation must fit with these as well. It must be an opportunity to live up to your responsibilities and keep a sense of belonging. It must be something that fits into the goals and hopes that form your motivations. Last, it must line up with the direction of your life: when you find your potential and understand a goal, you must find work that lets you pursue that.

Each of these qualities must be possible within your work for it to reach the status of vocation. All of this is united by the basic nature of work: it's an activity that we do for the sake of something greater. We work to bring an idea into reality. Here, the idea is the person you want to be.

We've emphasized time and time again that the real fulfillment of work comes when its goal is united with the rest of life. We've identified the broad goal of achieving your potential and becoming the person you're meant to be. Still, there's something more concrete to be found. We pursue potential for a reason. What are the ultimate goals of these pursuits? What is it that makes these things worthwhile? What's the real motivation behind all of this?

Seeking the Fundamental Goods

Vocation doesn't just mean what you do for work. It means finding your place in the world and learning where work belongs in your life. It's about choosing what you want to live for and how to use work to make that life a reality. What kind of goal could bring these together?

We know one thing: this needs to be an *internal* good. We're looking for something that's inherent to work and life, not something tacked on at the end of it.

When we considered the idea of leisure, we found a few things that serve to motivate us simply for their own sake. We pursue truth, beauty, and community without anything else as a motivation—each justifies itself.

Each of these is distinct. We can recognize them as motivations for certain things. A researcher looks for truth, an artist looks for beauty, or a charity worker serves the community. We could look at them as distinct motivations, each serving as a reason to do one thing or another.

But looking at them as entirely separate is a mistake. While these fundamental goods do stand apart, they're also unified. Each comes from the same place and points towards the same end.

Underneath all of these, we see the virtue of *justice* at play. We defined justice as the knowledge of what's owed to everything and everyone. It's understanding what the world *should* be. This is the practical dimension of justice: every time you're asking about the right thing to do, you're asking about how things should be. What does this person deserve? What are my responsibilities to the world around me?

But the practical use of justice only comes with a deeper understanding of the world. At its core, justice means understanding the natural order of things. It's about knowing where things belong and how they fit together. Practical justice can't exist without this philosophical understanding.

When we talk about truth, beauty, and community, we're pointing to this natural order of things. Each of these concepts means recognizing and appreciating the order of the world. Truth means learning about this natural order. The pursuit of truth means looking for how everything fits together. A scientist asking what law of nature makes atoms act a certain way is looking for an order to things. What explains these different behaviors? We can see all these different facts, but what links them?

As humans, we can't see the world as a collection of isolated incidents. We're always looking for patterns. We want to find the links between these different things and seek a unified order to everything we experience. The fulfillment of the pursuit of truth comes when we understand what principles make these observations fit together.

We shouldn't just limit this to facts of physics or chemistry. We're looking for order when we ask about human nature or life's meaning. We find it easiest to think about the world in teleological terms: what is the purpose of all these things?

But in this search for the natural order of things, we should also take a moment to appreciate just how elegantly everything fits together. Finding harmony and order creates a sense of awe. In finding truth, we come to better recognize *beauty*.

Whenever we recognize beauty, we're recognizing the same thing that we saw in truth. Now, however, it's about taking a moment to simply wonder at the world. It's about seeing the words of a poem fit together the right way, seeing how the trees in a valley all grow alongside one another, or hearing a song where each note comes together to create something so much greater than the sum of its parts. Finding beauty means recognizing and appreciating this order in things.

The philosopher Immanuel Kant once said that appreciating a beautiful thing means looking for a purpose in something that can't be explained by any simple purpose. It's easy to understand the "meaning" of a hammer or a bird's nest—they both have a useful purpose that we can understand through quick observation. When we look at things as objects to be used for a particular end, it's not difficult to understand this order. But what's the purpose of a sunset? What's the purpose of a painting? We can understand why the sun sets or how a painting was made. We can try to describe what makes them useful or necessary.

But no matter how many of these factual questions we answer, we're still left with a feeling that there's something more. There seems to be a purpose that we can't reduce to any fact. When you're drawn in by the beauty of something, you start to recognize this sort of purpose that can't be put into words. It overwhelms your understanding.

This feeling might invite restlessness. But it can also offer us a reason for calmness.. It's an invitation to simply appreciate the order of the world. Though it might not be obvious how this thing fits in with everything else, it's clear that it's still in harmony with everything—this alone is worthwhile.

Perhaps most importantly, we begin to recognize where we fit into the order of things. In the grand order of everything, each of us fits in. You have your place and your vocation. Here, we recognize *community*.

True community means understanding how each person fits alongside one another and how to achieve the best state of life for everybody. It's a matter of applying this same order to our own lives and the people around us.

Of course, this doesn't just mean finding what's right. It also means becoming an active part of making that order a reality. It's not enough to just say that each person belongs here or there and deserves this or that. Community is meaningless if it's not a call to action. It shows us how we should live and how we should treat those around us.

The roots of community come in understanding truth. The foundation of every community is human nature. We're brought together because we are naturally inclined to live together and cooperate. We can stay together because we develop the virtues that let us live well with others. It's easy to see how the virtues let us live in harmony: a few minutes with someone who has no self-control and no patience will show you just how necessary each of these skills is.

Everything that we do finds its ultimate purpose in these fundamental goods. We're motivated by these natural goods at work and at rest. Whatever we pursue, we can find these present somewhere within our actions.

Understanding these basic goods shows us just how the goals of work and life are connected. Whether you're trying to master a skill at your job or having a good conversation with a friend, these goods stay the same. They guide us at all times and offer a unified goal. We're always pursuing this basic order.

Now, we're just left with one question: what is the best way to pursue these goods in life?

The Good Life

In his book *Nicomachean Ethics*, Aristotle asked what the best sort of life was. He argued that it couldn't be a life spent pursuing simple pleasures or a life spent looking for fame and wealth. Both leave happiness out of your control, and neither seems to get at the root of what we live for.

Ultimately, he concluded that it must be the life of a philosopher. This life, he says, has the most direct relationship to things like truth and beauty. These are the goods that we pursue for their own sake. Philosophy lets us study these things most directly. Beyond that, it offers a level of control that can't be found in the life of politics. Instead of your happiness relying on the opinions of others, it relies on the unchanging nature of these naturally good things to bring you fulfillment and purpose.

Now, many philosophers have tried to say that philosophy is the best thing to devote your life to—we might think that they're a little bit biased. Yet there's something to be said for what Aristotle asks us to do with our lives: he wants us to focus on looking for truth in our lives. He wants us to pursue a life that is centered around virtue and beauty.

But for Aristotle, this was a very practical and personal work as well. It was addressed to his son Nicomachus. In some sense, we can interpret this as a long letter from a father to a son about how to lead a happy life. This philosophy may seem impractical and removed from normal life. Yet when we look more closely, we find something that's rooted in something real and purposeful. It begins with honest concern for another.

It's clear that not everybody can be a philosopher in the traditional sense. We can't spend all of our time in contemplation. But we can find this contemplation in our work: everything can join in the pursuit of truth, beauty, and community. The fact that we can work to change the world and bring our ideas to reality is something worth appreciating and sacrificing for. Good work is a partner to the pursuit of these values.

Vocation really means looking for beauty in everything: we look for beauty in work, in rest, and in life as a whole. We grow to appreciate the virtues of work, the goals work's directed towards, and the beauty of life that leads us to vocation.

Alasdair MacIntyre once said that a good life is spent searching for the meaning of the good life. Our lives aren't just defined by the goal we're after. We need to find meaning in the search. Real integration means learning to take on this search everywhere, at work and at rest. We grow to appreciate the virtues and beauty of work.

Perhaps this is the simplest definition of vocation: it's beautiful work. In work as in everything, we look for something that is incredible yet cannot be explained without telling a story. Vocation isn't something that's found in one moment: it's developed over a lifetime.

CHAPTER SUMMARY:

- Vocation is the work that lets a person live up to his or her place in the world.

- Vocational work brings together the ideas we've covered so far—dignity, virtue, identity, and freedom—to create a life with a unified, teleological direction.

- We find a unified direction for life by looking at the basic goods: truth, beauty, and community. These are values that we can recognize in every part of life and that offer worthwhile goals for every pursuit in life.

REFLECTION QUESTIONS:

- What do you recognize as the driving values in your life? What's most important to you among the pursuit of truth, beauty, and community?

- Think about your life story. How can your work help you live up to this?

- What does vocational work mean for you? Where do you believe you can find work that meets the need for purpose and lets you live up to your place in the world?

About the Authors

Chris Farls is a retired entrepreneur with multiple successes owning and operating small-to-midsize businesses. He recently co-founded The Vocation Project and is dedicated to helping others see their work as part of a meaningful life. He is a proud Catholic, husband, father and Army veteran, and holds Engineering and MBA degrees from Virginia Tech and Carnegie Mellon.

Patrick Cavanaugh Koroly co-founded The Vocation Project to help bring philosophical ideas to working life. He has previously worked as a writer and tutor helping underprivileged students in Pittsburgh. He earned a degree in philosophy and German at the University of Pittsburgh and has published essays on literature, history, and philosophy in several publications. Away from work, he is a dedicated member of his local Catholic community.

What is The Vocation Project?

The Vocation Project is a research and education collaboration focused on bringing insights from the world of philosophy to everyday life. Combining decades of experience in the workplace and years of study, Chris and Patrick have worked to make complex ideas accessible and applicable to work and life. Our goal is to use timeless principles to bring clarity and direction to working professionals and suggest practical solutions to put these ideas into action.

For more content on our philosophy of work, visit our website: thevocationproject.com.